ARTIFICIAL INTELLIGENCE IN AUTONOMOUS LANGUAGE LEARNING

AN EXPERT SYSTEMS APPROACH TO COMPUTER ASSISTED EFL SELF STUDY

By the same author

Controversies in ELT

The Fractal Approach to Teaching English as a Foreign Language

www.linguabooks.com

ARTIFICIAL INTELLIGENCE IN AUTONOMOUS LANGUAGE LEARNING

AN EXPERT SYSTEMS APPROACH TO COMPUTER ASSISTED EFL SELF STUDY

Maurice Claypole

LinguaBooks

Print edition: ISBN 978-1-911369-53-0
eBook edition: ISBN 978-1-911369-54-7

Third edition

Copyright © 1989, 2014, 2020 Maurice Claypole
Layout and design: Copyright @ 2020 LinguaBooks

A CIP catalogue record for this book is available from the British Library.

LinguaBooks
Elsie Whiteley Innovation Centre
Hopwood Lane
Halifax HX1 5ER
United Kingdom

www.linguabooks.com

It's so dreamy, oh fantasy free me.
So you can't see me, no, not at all.
In another dimension,
With voyeuristic intention,
Well secluded, I see all.

With a bit of a mind flip
You're into the time slip.
And nothing can ever be the same.

Richard O'Brien
Time Warp from *The Rocky Horror Show*

About the author

Maurice Claypole BA, MA (Lond), Cert Ed, MCIL, FCollT, AITI, PhD has enjoyed a long career in English language teaching, teacher development and translation. He is currently Director of LinguaServe Language Services based in Germany, where he has also lectured in Technical English at Pforzheim University and in Business English at Nuertingen University. He is a University of Cambridge Local Examiner for English as a Foreign Language, a member of the Chartered Institute of Linguists and a Fellow of the College of Teaching. As a translator, he is an associate member of the Institute of Translation and Interpreting and certified by the German Chamber of Commerce. Posts formerly held include chairman of the English Language Teachers Association Stuttgart (ELTAS) and member of the Committee of Management of the International Association of Teachers of English as a Foreign Language (IATEFL). Published works include **The Fractal Approach to TEFL**, a study of complexity and dynamism in language teaching, **Controversies in ELT**, a collection of essays taking a critical stance on a number of topics relating to the teaching of English and **Trade Union Interactive**, a web-based ESP program incorporating a task-based approach to real-life case studies. He has also instigated and worked on a variety of blended learning projects designed to integrate the classroom experience with a range of technologies, including e-learning, streaming video, Skype conferencing and virtual 3D worlds.

Abstract

Despite major advances in computer hardware generally and in software development techniques in areas such as technical troubleshooting and gaming, computer assisted foreign language learning applications have not kept pace with the general trend.

A review of the scope of software solutions available for autonomous language learning seen at an early stage of their development is taken as the background for an examination of the potential of artificial intelligence routines developed for other purposes to enhance the effectiveness of language learning applications and humanize the user experience.

In particular, a study of the interface between the technology of expert systems and the characteristics of natural language processing provides insights which in combination with the principles of object-oriented software development could eventually bring about a long-awaited breakthrough in the area of computer assisted self study programs specifically designed for the independent language learner.

CONTENTS

PART TWO

PART THREE

Preface to the third edition

Revisiting the topic of artificial intelligence some thirty years after I first set out my thoughts on the nature of natural language processing has been an eye-opening experience. Once again, we are experiencing a time of technological change when expectations run high and experts in the field have at their disposal a rapidly expanding range of development tools, content management systems and user interfaces. In many sectors, interactive voice-controlled systems are commonplace and everywhere, friendly digital voices provide us with day-to-day information through mobile devices in a way that seemed impossible only a decade or so ago. In the midst of this, language learners are faced with a sometimes bewildering choice of options and opportunities and yet the goal of interactively harnessing machine intelligence for the benefit of the autonomous language learner seems as elusive as ever.

The third edition of this book includes additions that reflect the most recent advances in technology, in particular concerning the popular perception of artificial intelligence. At the time of the second edition, it once again seemed that the dawn of a new age of intelligent, interactive software was upon us. Suddenly, commentators who had never concerned themselves with the capabilities and limitations of software-based solutions were waxing lyrical about artificial intelligence (now tellingly abbreviated to AI) and the impact it was having on our daily lives. Suddenly, the media abounded with reports of powerful algorithms taking charge of key activities previously carried out only by humans and once again, futuristic visions of world domination by computerised life-forms became a favourite subject for the science fiction genre. Indeed, the pseudo-sentient beings of the movie world are a far cry from the algorithms I discussed in the first edition of this book. To what extent the reality of computer-based language learning had changed in the intervening years, was, however, a different matter.

These observations remain true today. In some respects, digital learning environments have changed beyond recognition in a relatively short space of time, but in many respects, these changes are merely superficial, leaving underlying structures, concepts and assumptions unchanged and uncontested.

The purpose of this third edition, therefore, is to leave my original observations intact, whilst also looking behind the hype of recent developments in fields such as digital language processing, virtual reality and augmented learning. In particular, the emergence of mobile technologies has proved to be a great force for change. Smart phones and cloud computing provide ubiquitous access to media-rich digital information presented by virtual assistants, whilst social networks offer the potential benefits of a real-time collaborative environment. For the autonomous language learner, this opens up new opportunities, but also presents new challenges and to an extent leaves some old problems unresolved.

Halifax, April 2020

Preface to the second edition

It is fair to say that I thought more than twice before deciding to prepare a second edition of this study in the second decade of the twenty-first century. In view of the fact that the key research was carried out in the early days of computer assisted language learning (CALL), my first instinct was to consign the work to history. Before doing so, however, I consulted colleagues in the field who assured me that even in its original form the book still had something to say, and that in many ways it shed light not only on the state of CALL at an early stage in its development but on today's use of technology, too. What is startling is not what has changed in the interim, but the somewhat disturbing extent to which learning systems as I examined and envisaged them at the time are still in their infancy.

Further encouragement in this venture was provided by the announcement in March 2014 that the BBC's computer game version of *The Hitchhiker's Guide to the Galaxy*, one of the adventure games I referred to in my original study, has just been reissued with the text component virtually unchanged. Not only is the pace of change slower than we are sometimes willing to believe, but there are also lessons to be learned from glancing back in time to a view of the future which has only partly become the present.

Pforzheim, April 2014

PART ONE

The State of the Art of CAEFL Applications

Introduction

In his discussion of Lisp Machine Architecture, David C. Schwartz (1985) points out that a software paradigm shift is currently taking place, analogous to the hardware paradigm shift of the 1970's. The hardware paradigm shift resulted in manufacturers of large mainframe systems progressively scaling their products down through minis and superminis to microcomputers, so that personal computers were eventually able to run software with computing power comparable to that of previous mainframes.

In terms of software, the paradigm shift has led to programming techniques arising from research into artificial intelligence systems being codified and used in turn by an increasing number of systems programmers for a variety of advanced applications. This entails developing new methods of data representation in the form of knowledge that can be subjected to rational analysis as well as techniques for the symbolic, algorithmic and logical manipulation of data. Programming techniques have been developed which make it possible to solve more complex problems than hitherto possible and to construct man-machine interfaces far in advance of anything previously imaginable.

The present study considers the state of the art of software systems currently in use for the teaching of English as a Foreign Language (EFL), including bilingual systems in use in a non-English speaking country (NESC) and examines both practical applications and theoretical considerations in the light of current trends in software development techniques.

The book itself arises out of eight years' practical research and experiment into various methods used in the teaching of English as a Foreign Language to small groups and individual students in an independent, non-system bound environment, combined with a study of software techniques normally regarded as being outside the direct scope of CALL projects. Its purpose is to consolidate the knowledge and experience gained during this period and, moreover, to investigate and evaluate the methodology of systems currently available with a view to both assessing their usefulness and determining the possible implications for future developments.

Purpose and Method

This study opens with a brief discussion of the hardware and software combinations currently in use for the teaching and learning of English as a Foreign Language, a description of a selection of software solutions in widespread use and a discussion of the pedagogical principles on which they are based. This entails an analysis of the particular problems faced by the designers of CALL programs and the degree of success with which these problems have so far been overcome. Reference will be made to a variety of existing programs in the light of their particular pedagogical and psychological foundations and some suggestions for improvement will be made in the light of experience gained outside the field of computer assisted language learning.

Scope of Study

Since a purely abstract and theoretical analysis of the possible implementations of information technology in education might arguably be limited only by the borders of one's imagination and bear no relevance to day-to-day learning practice, the emphasis in the first part of this book is placed on such computer assisted language programs as are readily available for autonomous learning using widely available hardware systems (home and personal computers) to which learners currently have access. Since the study was carried out in West Germany, the focus in this section is on software available on the German market.

Both practical issues and psychological and educational principles will play an important part in the analysis of the various packages, since it is my aim to test their actual usefulness during implementation and to analyse their pedagogical and psychological framework within the context of other learning methods available to the individual learner.

The second part of the book will then establish a critical context by casting the net wider to include a discussion of more theoretical concepts and take into consideration developments and research at a more advanced level of implementation including artificial intelligence and object-oriented software design and development.

Background

The development of computers has seen their range extended from their original military and scientific roles to cover almost every aspect of daily life. Whereas only a few years ago, electronic data processing was the exclusive prerogative of large and wealthy institutions – governments, universities, banks, multinational corporations and the like, a personal computer or home computer is now within easy financial reach of most families in the industrialized west. In fact, there are so many systems aimed at precisely this private and individual market that it is extremely difficult for a beginner to select a suitable computer from the many different types on offer. The rapid development of the last five years may be seen in the positive light of technological achievement, and a lot has indeed been achieved in a very short time. However, from an educational point of view, it remains to be seen whether the rapid rate of growth has been an advantage or not. It is true that almost every household nowadays has a personal or home computer and that somewhere in the vast software library of the average user there can usually be found one or more so-called 'language teaching programs', but what is lacking is the evidence of a successful application of these programs.

Systems under Consideration

The general relationship between CALL applications and the various categories of hardware may be summarized as follows:

1. Mainframe system: consisting of a large central computer to which access may be obtained (often by means of a telephone line) from non-intelligent terminals and peripheral equipment. Whereas this was the original birthplace of CALL, its use in CAEFL is now largely restricted to universities and similar institutions.

2. Minicomputer: smaller than a mainframe, access usually limited to the terminals and peripheral equipment of the institution or company in which the central processor itself is situated. The terminals of such systems are usually non-intelligent. The main applications here are commercial or scientific use with very little relevance to CALL work.

3. Microcomputer: an independent computer incorporating processor, keyboard, monitor and storage system in one unit, not dependent on a remote processing unit. The CPU usually consists of an 8-bit or 16-bit microprocessor although 32-bit machines are becoming more

common at the time of writing. Generally speaking, micros can be subdivided into:

a) Personal Computers (PCs) originally intended for small scale commercial and scientific applications for which access to a powerful central processor or database is not required. Typical operating system: MS-DOS, typical high-level programming language: PASCAL. Recent developments involving the linking of PCs via a telephone line or within a closed network system are bringing the applications and functions of PCs closer to those of larger systems and by using an intelligent system in conjunction with a powerful host computer, they provide a flexible and cost-effective alternative to larger systems. PC networks are, however, in their infancy, and no applications are currently available for language learning which exploit the networking potential of PCs (e.g. central learner monitoring and task apportioning).

b) Home Computers (referred to below as HCs). In processing power, these are more modest than PCs but offer the advantages of ease of use and low-cost software, of which a wide range is available. HCs often feature high-resolution graphics and impressive sound effects, making them ideal games computers, and, although managerial and educational programs are available for home computers, their main application indeed lies in the games market. Typical programming language: BASIC. Some home computers can also be connected to host computers and mailbox systems by means of a telephone line, but no language teaching programs currently exploit this facility.

Since neither mainframe nor minicomputers are easily accessible to the average user, the first part of this study concentrates on the implementation of microcomputers in the field of human language learning, and specifically to the teaching of English as a foreign language in a non-English speaking environment. The linguistic environment under study is the Federal Republic of Germany, but the findings may relate to all situations in which a student is striving to learn English as a foreign language without the support of naturally occurring English language in his daily environment but with the potential assistance of computer technology and single or dual language teaching programs.

Acronyms

Previous literature often fails to distinguish clearly between CAI (computer assisted instruction) and CAL (computer assisted learning), probably because so little real use is made of either outside certain areas. In CAI, the computer is used primarily to impart information and issue guidelines for the user. An example of CAL, however, would be a flight simulator, in which the machine does not instruct, but provides the means for a trainee pilot to gain valuable flying experience. The acronym CALL (computer assisted language learning) has already been used (Higgins, 1984), and I have extended this further to read CAFLL (computer assisted foreign language learning) and more specifi-cally, CAEFL (computer assisted English as a foreign language), disciplines in which hitherto very little work has been carried out. Reference will also be made to CAESP (computer assisted English for special purposes), although the distinction here is more one of content than principle, since CAESP programs often differ from CAEFL programs only in the content of their data-bases. In the present work, I also use (sparingly) the terms CAEFLSS (computer assisted EFL self-study), ALL (autonomous language learning) and CAALL (computer assisted autonomous language learning).

CALL Applications

The last few years have seen such rapid advances in microcomputer technology that today's systems would have been scarcely imaginable some ten years ago and that the revolutionary breakthroughs of the early years now seem ridiculously primitive in comparison with today's technology.

Regrettably, the software available for CALL has not advanced as quickly as the hardware. One of the first commercially available home computers, the ZX 80, introduced as a world-beating innovation in 1980 had just 1 K of memory, enough to store about one page of program or information, in other words not even enough memory space to handle a convincing vocabulary quiz, let alone cope with the grammatical complications of a foreign language. Amazingly, this machine was marketed initially as a new form of learning aid, and the initial press advertisements depict the ZX 80 being used for clearly educative purposes, a claim still advanced by the manufacturers of much more advanced home computers despite the fact that marketing results show that HCs are now used primarily for games purposes. The built-in software of the ZX-80 was simplicity itself, too: it contained a BASIC interpreter that handled only integer arithmetic. Three divided by two was, according to the ZX-80, one. The system limitations clearly reduced its usefulness for serious language teaching programs. However, it was possible to produce simple programs, such as my 1981 routine for teaching how to tell the time in a foreign language, which I have reproduced and annotated in Appendix I.

There is only one single underlying idea behind this program: the user enters an answer and the computer compares it with the pre-programmed correct answer and declares the user's answer to be right or wrong. The computer also manages to keep score and inform the user of his progress. Not a brilliant concept, but about all that can usefully be achieved with only 1 K of memory. The hardware of the ZX-80 also had the disadvantage of an undersized foil keyboard lacking moving keys and requiring in many cases two or three keys to be pressed in sequence in order to achieve a particular effect whilst other command words could be obtained by pressing a single key – very complicated and confusing for the beginner and very unfamiliar for the professional user.

As the possibilities of the HC market were recognized by a growing number of manufacturers, the ZX-80 very quickly passed into history. It was followed by the ZX-81 (sold in the United States as the TS 1000), which achieved a global breakthrough a year later by being the first machine to conquer the HC market worldwide whilst still, however, sporting only a mere 3.5 K of random access memory.

Hardware

An easily affordable home computer now offers upwards of 64 K of RAM with three times as much again easily accessible on disk, whilst more expensive models currently offer 20- or 30-megabyte hard disks together with a wide of range of operating systems. HCs are available, such as the Commodore 128-D which offer a built-in disk drive, can be expanded to 640 K and operate optionally under CP/M, at which point the distinction between

HC and PC is a largely theoretical one. Similarly, the Amiga range offers graphics capabilities far beyond many PC systems. And whereas the ZX-80 and ZX-81 user struggled with a foil keyboard, options now available vary from the standard typewriter-style keyboard to the paddle, joystick, touch-pad and mouse, the latter largely removing the necessity to press keys or locate letters on the keyboard. All functions can be accessed by moving a small hand-held device across a tabletop. Speech digitiser have now been available for some time, and it is surely only a question of a few years before speech input/output routines make the micro a potentially valuable tool for the non-computer oriented language learner.

The present state of speech digitisers for the PC and HC is, however, quite primitive. Mechanical-sounding phoneme-based, or even letter-based speech synthesizers are available for HCs, whilst more sophisticated versions have been developed for the IBM-PC and compatibles. Typically, however, all these solutions are supplied with very little software support and cannot effectively be integrated into meaningful CAEFL programs. Furthermore, the memory requirements of human speech digitalization preclude its successful implementation on the existing range of HCs and PCs.

In terms of the system software available for micros, considerable advances have been made in the last few years. Better central processors have enabled software engineers to produce faster, more efficient programs and routines, to improve programming languages and to make systems much more user-friendly. Much improved toolkits are available (some of these will be discussed in Part Two) and a great many advances have been made in operating systems and programming languages.

On the other hand, in the HC market, some old favourites refuse to go away: the Commodore 64, statistically the most widely used home computer in the world (5 million sales worldwide by the Summer of 1989, of which 1 million were in West Germany alone), is not only still widespread throughout the country but remains a best seller in its price category. Many PC programs have been successfully adapted for the C-64 and, indeed, some software originally designed to utilize the polyphonic sound capabilities and Sprite graphics of the C-64 have had to be simplified for the ostensibly more powerful IBM-PC.

No advance has been as rapid as the games market. Whereas at the beginning of the 1980's the world was still being amazed by such games as *Pong* and *Space Invaders*, a mere two or three years later the graphic capability of machines such as the Commodore C-64 had been exploited to such a degree that the mere blips on the screen of the original television games seemed like relics from a kind of computer stone age, and at the time of writing, systems such as the Commodore Amiga are readily available which can display a digitalized image worthy of, and indeed often produced by, a video camera. In the last two or three years, the games market has, however, shown a levelling-off, although as regards CALL, student expectations are often raised by advance marketing and impressive advertising campaigns, expectations which are rarely fulfilled, being based on misconceptions about the nature of computer dialog and the state of the art of CALL programs. Above all, autonomous study requires discipline and/or strong motivation if successful learning is to take place amongst a non-captive user group. An inverse parallel may be drawn here to the proponents of Superlearning methods, who all seem to be aware of the need to convince the user that the system works before actually attempting to present lesson material. Evidence of this may easily be found in introductory texts to Superlearning (Suggesto-pedia) courses. First, the user's apprehensions are removed and a frame of mind conducive to learning with the system at hand is striven for. Presenters of pure software packages make no attempt to justify their use of computer technology nor indicate in what way the method of presenting the material may differ from the user's preconceptions. Most CALL systems today are, after all, technology-based rather than user-based.

The Genesis of Computer Assisted Language Learning

The first CALL systems were developed in universities for use with language undergraduates, an environment in which language teaching is predominantly concerned with traditional teaching methodologies which concentrate on vocabulary, grammar and translation. Little need was seen, and little effort was made, to deviate from the approach to the problems of language adopted in university language departments generally. For this reason, language teaching programs were developed which bore little relation to the actual practical requirements of second language learners in a non-university environment: evening-class students, private language school students, schoolchildren and interested individuals learning at home. Yet one of the great benefits of a mechanical tutoring system, whether it be a language laboratory booth, a home cassette course, a programmed book or a computer-based system, is individualization. Each student, or each user of a system, can work at his or her own speed and individual learners can deter-mine the course of instruction themselves, so that no time is wasted in unnecessary repetition and no individual difficulties are overlooked. However, whereas the progress of learning can generally be paced according to the requirements of each individual student, the learner is not in a position to influence the structure or flow concept of the learning package, the type of activity or the order in which material is learned.

This lack of user control is not necessarily a disadvantage in practice, since it is debatable whether or not the student is in the best position to make such decisions. Might a choice of activities not sometimes result in the student selecting the most interesting, or most amusing activities in preference to the most difficult and perhaps most needed?

Areas of CALL Implementation

In an evaluation of ten different CAL/CAI research projects, Kemmis et al. (1977) defined four areas in which computers can usefully be implemented. These may be summarized as follows:

1. Instructional
    Drill and practice, tutorial style 'involves the belief that the knowledge students need to acquire can be specified in language and learned by the transmission and reception of verbal messages.' In this learning paradigm, the subject matter is central to the teaching process.

2. Revelatory
    This approach concentrates on discovery and vicarious experience through simulation and data handling; key ideas are gradually revealed. This is similar to my notion of 'indirect' language teaching discussed below and in terms of CAEFL is the approach of such games programs as *Grammarland* (Higgins, 1984), *Leisure Suit Larry* and *King's Quest*.

3. Conjectural

   This emphasizes active knowledge, manipulation and hypothesis testing. 'People who work within this paradigm tend towards the view that knowledge is created through experience and evolves as a psychological and social process' (Kemmis et al., 1977).

4. Emancipatory

   This indicates the division of student activity into authentic and inauthentic labour, inauthentic labour being that which is incidental to the learning process, authentic labour that which is directly related to it (valued learning). An approach to CALL which enhances authentic labour and/or minimizes inauthentic labour falls into the category of emancipatory learning.

Roles of the Computer in CALL

In a language learning environment, computer hardware can be put to use in a variety of different ways, not all dependent on the availability of CALL-specific software tools:

1. As an electronic display unit

   In a teaching situation in which a human teacher is using HW technology as a teaching aid, the computer screen becomes, in effect, an electronic blackboard, used rather like an overhead projector. Used well, this can enhance the learning experience but may intrude upon the learning process if the means becomes a centre of attraction.

2. Monitoring

   The data storage facilities offered by even the most modest HC make it possible to keep a record of student progress, either for an individual's own guidance or for comparison with fellow students. By linking PCs in a network (a growing trend at the time of writing, particularly in schools, small businesses and similar institutions, although not yet discernible in the private, domestic sector), this facility could be extended to provide centralized monitoring of student progress and also, theoretically at least, to assist in optimizing the efficiency of subsequent release versions by analysing which program functions are used most frequently. There is, however, very little evidence of these facilities being adequately exploited.

3. As an individual resource

    The independent learner making use of school or college facilities may have access to stored data or tutoring functions analogous to those found in an audio library or language laboratory. At home, an HC or PC may be used as a personal database in which to record lesson information acquired by other means or as a retrieval system for commercially available information packages. The computer is, in this case, assuming the role of an electronic library shelf.

4. Group activity

    In much the same way as modern arcade games may be played either by each player individually against the machine or as a direct contest of skill between players using the machine as an electronic games board, so too can language games be constructed which provide additional stimulus to language learning situations by adding an extra element of competition. A game such as Hangman can, for example, be played as a pair, group or individual activity. Since our main focus is on independent learners, the language-oriented games we will consider in this context have been selected to reflect an emphasis on individual student-machine interaction and competition.

5. Direct stimulus

In a classroom situation, the computer can be used to stimulate discussion in the foreign language, usually at a fairly advanced level. In this model, the computer merely provides linguistic stimulus in form of text or questions and becomes a kind of talking point. As with Hangman or adventure games, the participation of a teacher can complement the activity of the computer and compensate for its shortcomings. However, this technique is only possible in the presence of a teacher or experienced group leader. The act of reading aloud from the screen may take on an important role here, and if only one input device is used, discussion is stimulated when other students are obliged to give direct instructions to the user. Clearly, this is a very limited application which is more dependent for its success upon the interaction between humans than upon the nature of the man-machine interface. A further discussion of such group activities therefore falls outside the scope of the present study.

Notional/Functional Language Teaching

Language syllabuses are often conceived as a list of linguistic elements which can be clearly defined, such as grammatical structures, lexical sets and semantic equivalents, based on the assumption that if the full syllabus of these items is taught and learned then the pedagogical goal of language acquisition is attained. Such tasks would seem to fall within the scope of computer technology, at least theoretically. However, more recent developments in language teaching, such as notional/functional syllabuses, are less easy for a computer programmer to handle. Notional/functional teaching activities are based on the idea that the language required for a specific communicative function should be taught as required in order to achieve communication rather than in order to exemplify a particular grammatical construction. Thus, greetings may be taught in an initial contact phase regardless of the linguistic structures involved. Such a task is much more difficult for the computer programmer to simulate and the direction taken by the language interaction is almost impossible to anticipate. Similarly, 'deep-end teaching', imposing a task on the learners and then correcting as necessary and finally asking them to repeat the original exercises with the newly acquired resources, is not within the range of the present generation of CALL software solutions.

In my own language teaching, whether with groups or individual students, I often employ a technique which I like to refer to as the 'indirect method' as a means of distinguishing this classroom technique from the 'direct' method of the late sixties. Seen from the teacher's point of view, it is inductive rather than instructive in nature and has at its root the question rather than the statement. From the student's point of view, the learning process is a revelatory one, combining empirical knowledge with heuristic thought process, pre-knowledge and guesswork. On a simplistic level, for example, one could react conventionally to a student's query about the meaning of a word, say, 'car ferry', with a translation, a definition or an explanation.

Possible responses would therefore be:

1. 'It means 'Autofähre'.'

2. 'It's a boat used for transporting passengers and vehicles between two ports.'

3. 'If you go from Calais to Dover, you usually take the car ferry.'

An indirect (inductive) response, however, would be in the form of a question which would allow the student to arrive at the answer on the basis of his or her existing knowledge base, e.g.

1. 'How do you normally cross from Calais to Dover?'

2. 'What do you call a boat that travels to and fro between two points?'

3. 'Do you know any ways of transporting a car?'

Usually, a sequence of such questions is required in order to eventually elicit a response from the student that shows that they have finally understood the subject matter at hand. Of course, the human language teacher has many more resources than mere language manipulation (intonation, gesture, impromptu sketches, classroom props, etc.), but it is the language element that is of interest to us here. Admittedly, a certain degree of patience and skill is required on both sides, but successfully implemented, this technique produces lasting and satisfying results. I term this method 'indirect' because the actual subject matter being taught is not the ostensible content of the dialog at all, but the skills of understanding and questioning which are incidental to it.

Language Learning and Language Acquisition

Stephen Krashen (1982) has argued that there is a distinction between 'language learning' and 'language acquisition'. According to Krashen, the brain utilizes language which is learned (I would refer to this as cognitive learning) and language which is acquired (in my view this can be either empirical or heuristic learning) separately, and there is little interchange between the two. The acquisition store is used for the creative and spontaneous use of language, whereas the learning store is limited to mental translation and acts as a monitor on the language produced by the acquisition store, providing for error correction. This implies that language can only effectively be acquired in the presence of an environment in which the learner is exposed to a range of language patterns beyond his or her immediate comprehension. This kind of immersion learning dispenses with traditional teaching techniques such as behaviourist drills and notional/functional practice routines. It would appear that this kind of immersion is beyond the scope of microcomputers, but ironically, it is precisely in this area that a great deal of language teaching activity currently takes place, although not by means of language-teaching programs in the first instance. Rather it is a spin-off effect of adventure games such as *CIA Adventure*, *Star Trek* and *King's Quest* that comes closest to realizing the goals of both Krashen's concept of language acquisition and that of notional/functional teaching.

Krashen's notion of acquisition learning is, in fact, not far removed from the revelatory paradigm discussed earlier. Revelatory (acquired) knowledge is empirical, whereas 'learning' a language is a purely cognitive process. In foreign language learning, probably more than in any other subject, acquired skills are of paramount importance and yet they are often underemphasized, taking second place to cognitive skills (vocabulary learning, grammatical rules, etc.), and for this reason, interactive (revelatory) software solutions are the ultimate goal.

The State of the Art of CAEFL Software

The majority of CAEFL programs consist mainly or exclusively of vocabulary trainers. Ancillary functions vary but differ only minimally from program to program. *Exercise-Plus* from the Kay Laukat Verlag offers 3,000 lexical items divided into 12 vocabulary lessons of 5 blocks each. The student can select between a 'learning' function in which lexical items are displayed at random with their German translations, or a 'test' function in which the student is asked to provide the translations (in either direction). Progress statistics are continuously displayed, and provision is made for 'against the clock' exercises. The initial vocabulary of 3,000 words is somewhat modest but can be expanded by the user. Two interesting features of this particular program, however, are the addition of 2,400 complete expressions and a spelling checker. Add-on packages are available to adapt the basic kernel to CAESP purposes, namely in the fields of general technical and commercial English. Text books are supplied to support the screen-based lessons.

The majority of vocabulary-based CAEFL programs suffer from an inadequate knowledge base, offering either only single translations and/or containing an unacceptable number of mistakes. *SAA*, however, offers a dictionary incorporating a completion text editor and DOS shell containing some 30,000 words, whilst *TRANSLATE* from Brodowski offers 44,000 plus a vocabulary trainer. One of the most useful dual language spelling checkers currently available in the Federal Republic of Germany is a Swiss product, *Witchpen Combi*, which offers 180,000 words in each language, expandable to one million words and is supplied as a resident background routine for incorporation into word processing systems. Since both the spell checker and the translation functions can also be accessed from the DOS commando line, the shell could easily be incorporated into a vocabulary training program. However, at the time of writing no such applications are commercially available.

Language-Master PLUS

As a typical example of a cognitive-based tutoring program, here is an extract from one of the most widespread of English-language teaching programs in Germany, *Language-Master PLUS* from P. Herzog Software. It is presented here as a representative example of the current state of English language teaching software available for the PC. The main difference between the various programs currently available in this market is the number of lexical items contained in the data files. I have selected *Language-Master PLUS* for detailed examination not because it is the best, nor indeed the worst program currently available, but because it is the most representative from a point of view of functions offered, user-friendliness, linguistic content and pedagogical awareness. As will be seen, the program is easy to use, contains an extremely useful vocabulary set for the beginner, based on the principle of direct German/English equivalents, and provides some basic practice in using key structures together with a model-oriented presentation of new or revision material. As will also be seen, the program is, however, sadly lacking when put to the test, providing neither variety, dialog, linguistic reliability nor, in any real sense, instruction or teaching.

The program is quite easy to use, and the screen presentation is carefully thought out and clearly arranged. When used with an appropriate monitor, colour and inverse characters are exploited to good effect to enhance the various functions. Menu selection is quite user-friendly, although there are no on-screen help menus available. The screen-by-screen program description which follows is intended to show how the user interacts with the software, beginning with the initial start screen (assuming that all files have previously been installed on a hard disk). The standard PC keyboard is the sole input device and the output is entirely monitor-based without provision for a printout of either the vocabulary items, the exercises stored in the data files or the student's progress. No provision is made for use by more than one student, nor are interrupted or complete learning sessions stored for subsequent continuation or reference. (Some programs, such as *Brush up Your English* from Data Becker, offer this function, recording each individual student's progress and building a student-oriented file of learned vocabulary items and mistakes previous made.)

Program Description

The program actually consists of a package of individual sub-programs handled by means of a simple menu management system. The version under test offered the following features:

1. Memory-resident dictionaries (German to English and English to German) containing approx. 20,000 headwords for use outside the teaching program environment. Resident dictionaries must be installed

separately from the main program (see file listing below).

2. Resident and non-resident dictionaries can be expanded by the user on the basis of one-to-one equivalences between source and target language.

3. Automatic recognition of storage medium (e.g. hard disk, floppy) with automatic disk change prompt suppression in the case of a hard disk and automatic return to the distribution menu between program options.

4. Pop-up menus and windows together with colour identification of source or target language and highlighting where appropriate; blinking characters to indicate when computer is presenting solutions to an exercise.

5. 'Vocabulary Tutor', English-German

6. 'Vocabulary Tutor', German-English

7. 'Language Tutor', incorporating reading texts, explanatory screens and completion exercises

8. Irregular verb tutor

9. Dictionary, English-German

10. Dictionary, German-English

11. Session score and evaluation

12. High score storage

13. Dictionary correction routine

On calling up the program, the following options are offered to the user:

VOCABULARY TUTOR ENGLISH-GERMAN

VOCABULARY TUTOR GERMAN-ENGLISH

LANGUAGE TUTOR I

END PROGRAM

All headings and screen instructions are in German. Menu selection is by means of cursor controls. The screen display highlights the selected option by in inverse characters. The version on test offered some 7,400 lexical items, not a comprehensive vocabulary but much better than some competing products. However, unlike some programs (e.g. *Brush up Your English* from Data Becker), the quiz function does not ask for synonyms or provide definitions, but merely requires one-to-one translations of individual words. Similarly, the 'help' function does not provide text hints but merely offers one letter of the solution for each incorrect keystroke.

The verb trainer offers two out of three of: infinitive, preterite and past participle, requiring the user to supply the third form.

Fig. 1 shows the user interface of the *Language-Master PLUS* vocabulary trainer. In this example, the learner is being asked to enter a German translation for the English word 'truant'.

```
Language-Master PLUS  V 1.2   ELEKTRONISCHES WÖRTERBUCH   Englisch/Deutsch

    Zu übersetzender Begriff:          Highscore :    500

                                       Punkte :        10
          truant
                                       Noch 47 Abfragen...

    Ihre übersetzung :                 Hilfestellung :

          schwank                          schwä

  Begriff übersetzen
  Vokabeltrainer
  Unregelmäßige Verben
  Begriff korrigieren
  Vokabular erweitern
  PROGRAMM VERLASSEN
                      Lernen der gespeicherten Vokabeln
```

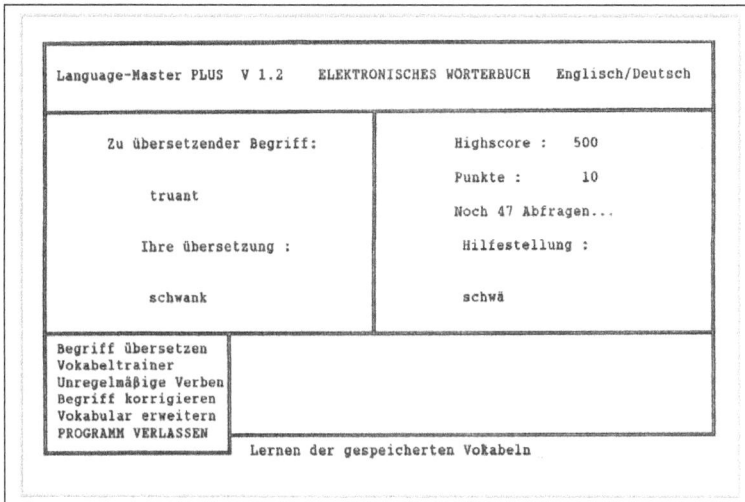

*Fig. 1. Typical screen from Language-Master PLUS showing the
Quiz and Help functions*

In the translation function, the user may enter a headword
which is then translated, provided that the headword is unique.
If this not the case, or if the headword itself also forms the initial
part of any other source language words, whether cognate or
not, these are all displayed. Thus, on a random test, entering the
English word 'impudent' produced one possible translation,
'unverschämt', whilst 'imp' produced no correct translation, but
the following list spread over five screens:

impair	=	beeinträchtigen
impart	=	verleihen
impartial	=	unparteiisch
impassable	=	unbefahrbar

39

impatience	=	Ungeduld
impeach	=	anklagen
impediment	=	Hindernis
impel	=	antreiben
impend	=	bevorstehen
imperative	=	befehlend
imperceptible	=	unmerklich
imperfect	=	unvollkommen
imperious	=	herrisch
imperishable	=	unvergänglich
impersonal	=	unpersönlich
impertinent	=	unverschämt
impervious	=	unzugänglich
impetuous	=	ungestüm
implacable	=	unversöhnlich
implement	=	Gerät
implicit	=	inbegriffen
implore	=	erflehen
imply	=	andeuten
impolite	=	unhöflich
import	=	Einfuhr
important	=	wichtig
importunate	=	zudringlich
impose	=	aufbürden
impossibility	=	Unmöglichkeit
impostor	=	Betrüger
impracticable	=	unausführbar
impregnate	=	imprägnieren
impress	=	Eindruck
imprint	=	prägen
imprison	=	einkerkern
improper	=	unpassend

improve	=	verbessern
improvise	=	improvisieren
imprudent	=	unklug
impudent	=	unverschämt
impulse	=	Anstoß
impunity	=	Straflosigkeit
impure	=	unrein
impute	=	zuschreiben

As this list also demonstrates, the program suffers badly from an inadequate knowledge base. Incorrect and misleading translations are common and there are a number of surprising omissions (e.g. 'impossible'). A function is available to expand and correct these entries, but this is of little use to the autonomous learner.

The comprehension tests supplied consist of both dialogs and narratives divided into strict lessons, each followed by an extremely short grammar section and a completion exercise. The standard is comparable with state school books, but the context is somewhat thin. Here is a sample dialog from lesson one of the five supplied:

A: *Hello, Janet! What a surprise!*

B: *Hallo, Sandra! Nice to see you. How are you?*

A: *Oh, fine, thanks. And you?*

B: *I'm very well too, thank you. But how's your father? Is he in hospital?*

> A: No, he isn't. He is quite well again. His leg is much better. But he's alone at the moment. My mother is in Ireland with her sister.
>
> B: Oh, is she? - Well, I'm glad your father is all right. Please give him my regards. – There's my bus at last. Good-bye for now!
>
> A: Bye, Janet! All the best!

This not very convincing dialog is followed immediately by a grammar screen which aims to teach by example and translation only, offering short model sentences (e.g. 'What is YOUR name?' together with German translations. Such techniques clearly do not exploit the interactive potential of even a PC or HC, but are techniques borrowed from, and more appropriate to, written material.

It is also of interest to note that several of the newer CAEFL packages are now accompanied by written course material, an implicit admission by the manufacturers themselves that the current software approach to CAEFL is in some respects lacking.

As an indication of the standard aimed at by *Language-Master PLUS*, two screens from the fifth and final lesson are reproduced below. Fig. 2 shows part of the study text, which is spread over three consecutive screens, following which the student has the option to review the complete text. There is, however, no facility for browsing between screens during display. The student can only go back to the beginning and start again.

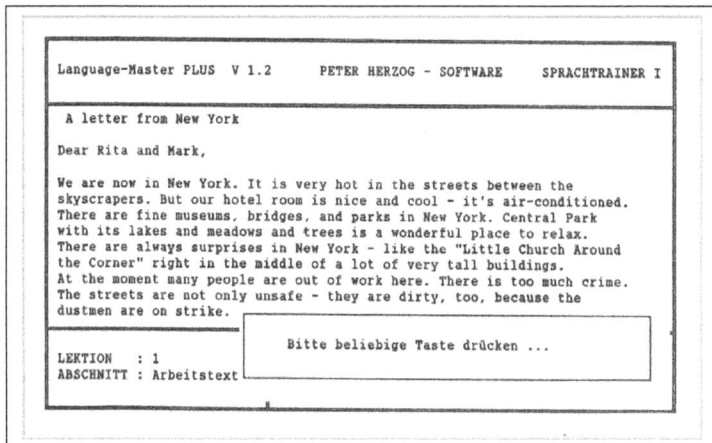

Fig. 2. Extract from typical Study Text, Language-Master PLUS

Finally, Fig. 3 shows the corresponding completion exercise:

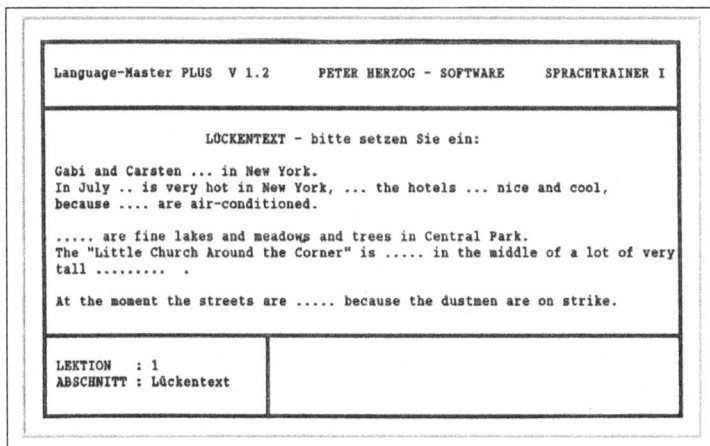

Fig. 3. Sample completion exercise from Language-Master PLUS

When the student has made his or her entries, the program fills in the correct version, erasing the student's own attempts. Thus, learners working alone cannot identify their mistakes; they can merely return to a specific section at a later time.

At the end of the session, the student is given a simple statistical analysis in the form of number of problems set and number of correct answers, together with a grading.

Programmed Learning

The *Language-Master PLUS* program is clearly limited by the software developer's (or the development team's) knowledge of English (and here the programmer quite clearly makes mistakes) and by the necessity to compare the student's answer to pre-programmed solutions. The teaching method used is one of test-check-reinforce, a throwback to the behaviourism of the nineteen fifties and sixties. Neither the language laboratory boom nor the introduction of 'programmed books' and 'tutor-texts' have withstood the test of time for reasons which with hindsight might seem obvious. The combination of behaviourism as a pedagogical principle and structuralism as a linguistic one, together with the impersonal nature of the hardware itself, seems to have been doomed to failure. Schools and other educational establishment invested in hardware whilst the software (at that time the language tapes and support material available) were underdeveloped, misconceived and primitive.

It seems inconceivable that these mistakes could be repeated, and yet that is what the evidence of recent years would suggest, with the difference that now not only schools and colleges are getting caught in this trap, but individual learners, too, who initially are led by hardware and software manufacturers to believe that they can learn a language without the support of a human teacher by using their home or personal computer. Research does not bear out this claim.

The real lessons of the fifties and sixties do not seem to have been learned by the software designers of the nineteen eighties who are often happy to produce a program which can identify isolated elements of natural language and compare them with memory-resident chunks regardless of context. The majority of programs available today either teach by translating individual words or provide practice by setting completion exercises or verb tests with statically pre-determined fixed answers.

By setting problems for the student and then providing the 'right' solutions, the program author is toeing a precarious line between assessment (verifying and recording the learning that has already taken place by other means) and teaching by the presentation of facts (CAI). The basis for learning being assumed here is not all that far removed from Thorndike's Law of Effect ('responses that have satisfying consequences are repeated...') and Skinner's notion of operant conditioning, directing the student towards the pre-determined goal, in this case the acquisition of vocabulary (knowledge). However the question-response mode of procedure requires the addition of a further concept in order to be effective, that of feedback, so that the full pattern should become question-response-feedback, which in turn should determine the next question or problem. The latter procedure is well within the technical limitations of modern microcomputers, and yet no effective programs are currently available which exploit this aspect of 'programmed learning'. Furthermore, it is neither pedagogically satisfying nor an efficient use of resources to merely inform students if their answers are right or wrong. It would be far more effective to develop algorithms in which each learner's individual responses become a control factor co-determining the structure of the learning program by selectively sequencing the program flow.

This more dynamic approach entails a certain amount of built-in redundancy, since students would automatically skip some material, but as storage becomes cheaper and more readily available, it would be preferable to expecting or requiring each autonomous learner to follow the same learning path. Furthermore, suitable user interface control mechanisms already exist. Even multiple-choice quizzes can perform this function, and attempts have already been made to use a similar form of response parsing in printed teaching material. Fig. 4 shows an extract from a recent textbook designed to teach the fundamentals of CMOS technology.

14. Either electrons or holes can be attracted into the channel region, depending upon whether a positive or negative potential, respectively, is applied to the insulated gate electrode. Remember that opposites attract. A positive charge on the gate electrode will attract _____ into the _(electrons/holes) channel region.	*electrons*
15. You will recall that MOS transistors are unipolar and thus conduct current using either positive (hole) or negative (electron) charge carriers—but not both at the same time. MOSFET's that utilize electrons to conduct current in the channel are known as N-CHANNEL devices. Similarly, transistors using holes for conduction are called P-CHANNEL devices. When an MOS transistor operates by virtue of a POSITIVE gate potential attracting ELECTRONS in the channel region, it is known as a(n) _____ channel device. _(p/n)	*n*
16. There are two types of MOS devices: n-channel (_____ _____), and p-channel (_____ _____).	*electron conduction, hole conduction*
17. Listed below are four possible types of MOS transistors. Which type(s) are employed in CMOS circuits? (CHECK ALL THAT APPLY) _____a. N-Channel Enhancement _____b. N-Channel Depletion _____c. P-Channel Enhancement _____d. P-Channel Depletion	*a. and c.*
18. In order to allow current to flow in a p-channel enhancement MOS transistor, it is necessary to apply a _____ voltage to the gate. _(positive/negative)	*negative* *(If you missed this one, review frames 13 a*
19. In contrast to CMOS logic, which uses both n- and p-channel transistors, some logic series use transistors of only one channel type. For example, NMOS refers to logic circuitry using only n-channel MOS transistors. A logic structure using only p-channel MOSFETS's would be called _____ .	*PMOS*

Fig. 4. Extract from programmed learning textbook on CMOS technology

Clearly, the underlying pedagogical principles of programmed learning textbook of this kind are rather primitive ones, and the activity required of the student is of a very limited and mundane nature. Neither in this example nor in the computer programs under analysis does discovery learning take place. In the case of the written example, both reinforcement and feedback are absent and as far as the programs are concerned, reinforcement is limited to praise from the machine, which is used sparingly, as indeed it should be, since too much praise from a clearly non-intelligent machine could easily be regarded as degrading and demeaning to its human user. The result is that the student very quickly becomes bored with the whole process and, lacking further reinforcement or motivation, subsequently elects not to use the program again.

In the PL approach there is no real communication, no dialog, no genuine linguistic interchange between the user and the machine. There are, however, a large number of adventure games currently available for many home computers in which a dialog between the user and the (not particularly bright) computer actually takes place. These games are not usually classed as teaching/learning games and indeed were written mainly as entertainment for native English speakers, but they also have a certain value as language teaching programs when used by non-native speakers. Currently, the most popular of these in the FRG are *Leisure Suit Larry* and *King's Quest*, both from Sierra Software. As a representative example of this kind of program, let us take game *King's Quest* in the version supplied for the IBM-PC.

In this game, the player converses with an automated partner, giving them instructions, which the partner then carries out in an attempt to achieve a specific goal. The on-screen dialog is supported by graphics showing the main character (Gwydion) and his environment, initially a magician's house seen through cut-away walls. Previous versions of this kind of game had required a linguistic input to initiate movement (e.g. 'Go North', 'Look Left', 'Enter'), but in the version under test, the cartoon-like character can be moved by means of cursor keys or mouse. Other instructions, however, must be entered on the keyboard. The character is then seen to respond, if appropriate, or the computer responds to the user's input by providing messages or warnings. Incidental activity, such as the appearance of the magician or his cat, occur on screen without prompting from the user. In contrast with earlier adventure games, it is not always the user who initiates the dialog.

Since a great deal of time and patience is required in order to ascertain the linguistic competence and limitations of the program, it is essential that a game, once commenced, can be stored, for example on a disk, for play to continue at a later stage. Interest would very soon flag if the user had to begin from the same point each time.

Sample Games Dialog Program - King's Quest

Program Selection

The program selected for testing and evaluation was *King's Quest III*, Version 2.00 by Sierra Software, released May 25, 1987. This program is not offered as a teaching program, but is designed as an adventure game in which the player assumes the role of a cartoon-type character displayed on the screen who can interact with his environment in two ways: by moving a fictional character within the screen environment using the cursor keys or a mouse, and through direct language input at the keyboard. It is the latter function which is of interest in the context of CALL because the actual linguistic interchange generated is comparable to some of the goals set by teaching and learning programs and in its conceptuality, the game is actually superior to many dedicated CALL programs. Furthermore, it embodies a random element which helps to eliminate the boredom that can result from the presentation of static, predetermined content.

Program Description

The game program incorporates the following basic functions:

1. High-quality graphics

2. Rudimentary sound output

3. Constant display of player's score

4. Constant display of game time elapsed

5. Pause function

6. Game storage and retrieval

7. NL (Natural Language) input parsing

8. Response to text input

9. Random machine action

10. Variable game parameters (sound, speed, etc.)

Appendix II reproduces an extract from the initial dialog between a human user and the supposedly omniscient computer charged with monitoring the fate of the user's character. The user is not familiar with the program and has never used a similar one before but has a reasonable command of conversational English. The adventure games approach differs from that of the *Language-Master PLUS* program in that it is largely up to the user to initiate each sequence of linguistic exchange. For the most part, it is the user who asks the questions or gives the commands, not the machine. So, although the machine is following a strict algorithm dependent on the user's inputs and certain random factors, for the user's part, they are encouraged to adopt a heuristic approach in order to determine which responses are 'correct'. On the one hand this contributes to the feeling that the human user and not the computer is in charge and on the other hand the computer can now no longer conceal the fact that it is a moron with a very poor grasp of English vocabulary and virtually no idea of grammar. In the example quoted, a clear deterioration of the user's level of English is perceptible, as they realize that the machine responds equally to, for example, 'look at the table' and 'look table'. Similarly the student's attempt to use their native word for a spoon unleashed a series of misunderstandings when they took the machine's response, expressed in question form, somewhat too literally.

Despite these shortcomings, students have often commented to me that the sheer entertainment value of text-based adventure games makes them a far more useful learning tool than actual CALL programs, and although the learning that actually takes place is mostly in the area of passive skills, the need to understand the computer's instructions and dialog outputs in order to complete the quest can be highly motivating. As a result, the user is benefiting from excellent reading comprehension practice, probably without even being aware of it. Furthermore, the graphic enhancement is itself conducive to vocabulary expansion. Each description of an object (e.g. the knife or the spoon in the sample run) is accompanied by an easily recognizable graphic representation of the object blended into the main screen as a window, a device many CALL vocabulary tutors could benefit from.

As a result of the low linguistic level of interaction in this particular program, however, the user is usually satisfied if his prompt is recognized and acted upon by the computer, regardless of whether it is linguistically correct or not. Once the user has found the right vocabulary, the linguistic part of the problem is, in fact, solved. Some words are 'right' and some are 'wrong' in exactly the same way that the vocabulary parsing routines in the *Language-Master PLUS* program accepted right answers to vocabulary tests and rejected wrong ones. However, at any particular point in the program there are a variety of linguistic inputs which are acceptable, just as there are in a real-life situation. Adventure programs vary in this feature. The more basic ones often fail to accept alternative vocabulary (e.g. 'put down' instead of 'drop'), but even with a selection of alternatives, the user very quickly learns to restrict his language to a few staccato keywords – not very conducive to the achievement of linguistic fluency. This disadvantage is, however, a limitation of the state of the art in natural language processing rather than a negative feature of games programs when used as a teaching aid.

The main attraction of adventure games as far as language acquisition is concerned probably lies in the very fact that the language activity itself is secondary to the immediate goal, i.e. to score points, solve the task or win the game. Language is here for once being used in its real context as a means to an end rather than an end in itself.

Such games are available entirely in the form of text dialog or, as discussed above, accompanied by graphics showing the current state of the game. Often, too, they use a form of language appropriate only within a very limited context, conversing in either pseudo-modern space language ('hyperspace jump', 'Arcturian Sector', 'Pan Galactic Gargle Blaster' – *The Hitchhiker's Guide to the Galaxy*) or in a quasi-historical form of English ('Which sword wouldst thou?' – *Sword of Fargoal*).

Many of these programs are available for low-end home computers and are indeed often designed specifically for such machines. It would therefore be unrealistic to expect too much sophistication from the hardware involved, but in my view, such programs must be viewed alongside official CAEFL programs as having great potential for harnessing existing technology to enhance foreign language learning.

It is my argument, therefore, that the deficiencies of adventure games for teaching purposes lie in the knowledge base rather than in their principle or design. A fairly primitive NL parsing technique may in fact be adequate to reach the goal of providing linguistic practice and improving the correctness and fluency if their knowledge base is expanded to accept a reasonable number of alternative user inputs and responses. However, the knowledge base of even such a program as discussed above is large enough to produce extended comprehension texts for the student, who needs to understand the screen text (gist or detail comprehension, as the case may be), in order to solve the puzzle. Indirectly, this also results in a high degree of passive vocabulary expansion. The next stage, then, is to extend the range and abilities of the NL interface so that a machine-oriented metalanguage of the type discussed is neither necessary nor acceptable.

The Role of the Software Engineer

In a domestic situation, one of the first questions an inquisitive visitor asks on seeing a home computer is 'What can it do?' This usually elicits a long list of the computer's practical and theoretical capabilities from its proud owner. I ask a similar question when I teach introductory courses in information technology, but usually in order to elicit a much different answer: nothing, or at best, very little. The computer itself obviously cannot do anything at all without clear instructions. Traditionally, it is the software engineer's task to deconstruct the task at hand into computer-operable tasks, determining what can and what cannot be achieved by the technology available, and then enable the computer to be used as a tool to reach the goal that has been set, or at least to come as close as the technical limitations will allow.

Subsequently, it is the user's (in the case of autonomous CAFLL, the student's) task to reach a specific goal by using the tools that the software engineer has provided, whether this goal is controlling a production machine or increasing proficiency in a human language. The computer may give the appearance of acting independently, but this is an illusion which is very soon shattered by practical experience at a keyboard. Thus, the general steps involved in producing a software solution are as shown below (Fig. 5).

```
        1.  Task analysis

        2.  Decomposition    ←─────────────────┐
                                               │
    ┌→  3.  Coding  ←───────────────────┐      │
    │                                   │      │
    └── 4.  Testing                     │      │
                                        │      │
        5.  Debugging  ─────────────────┘      │
                                               │
        6.  Prototype Release                  │
                                               │
        7.  Initial Implementation ────────────┘

        8.  Commercial Release

        9   Final Implementation
```

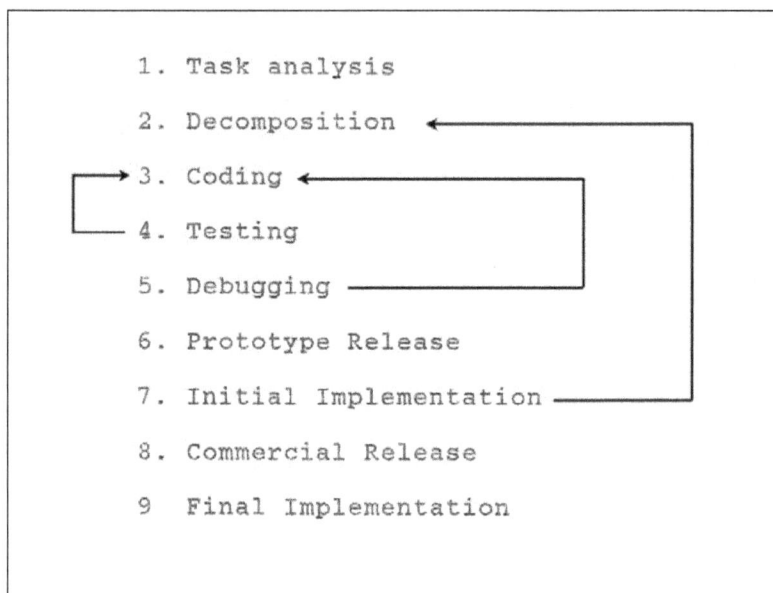

Fig. 5. Key stages of the software development process

Whereas stages two through seven of this model are to varying degrees recursive, it is my view that the majority of CALL systems are already doomed to failure at stage one and are therefore beyond salvation by further development, testing and modification. In other words, the wrong task is often specified at the outset, making the whole exercise a waste of time. Students will not improve their ability to communicate effectively in a foreign language by answering vocabulary quest-ions. They may, of course, improve their vocabulary, but it is questionable whether this is the key requirement of the average learner. By using a verb trainer one may learn that the past participle of 'buy' is 'bought', but this gives no indication of when to use it. Thus we return to the question of knowledge acquisition versus linguistic proficiency. Often, the argument is put forward that branching and checking is what the computer is good at, and therefore this is what it must be used for. Little effort has hitherto been made in CAEFL to set new goals and develop processing tools that are equal to the new tasks

Multiple Choice Quizzes

The computer is a tool and like any tool may be used or misused. A bad workman blames his tools and a good workman compensates, but any workman, good, bad or indifferent, reserves each of his tools for a specific task or group of tasks and uses them in turn to achieve a result. So the software engineer, having decided on his near objective (e.g. to produce a vocabulary quiz), must then achieve this under the constraints of the system they are using. The result is usually an algorithm on the lines of the multiple-choice model shown in Fig. 6.

Many reasonably efficient CAEFL routines exist which are based on this kind of model. However, such a solution assumes that the software designer and the subsequent user agree as to what the end-goal is, which must not be confused with the programmer's short-term objective. If the ultimate goal is skills acquisition, then the purpose is not served by a multiple-choice quiz of any degree of subtlety. The user may in fact have problems to which a heuristic rather than an algorithmic approach is more appropriate. But whereas the heuristic approach is arguably man's strong point, it is certainly not the machine's. At the present state of technology, the computer requires strict algorithms in order to simulate dialog and natural language. Its strength lies in its ability to consistently apply fixed rules during a decision-making process, not in trial-and-error techniques.

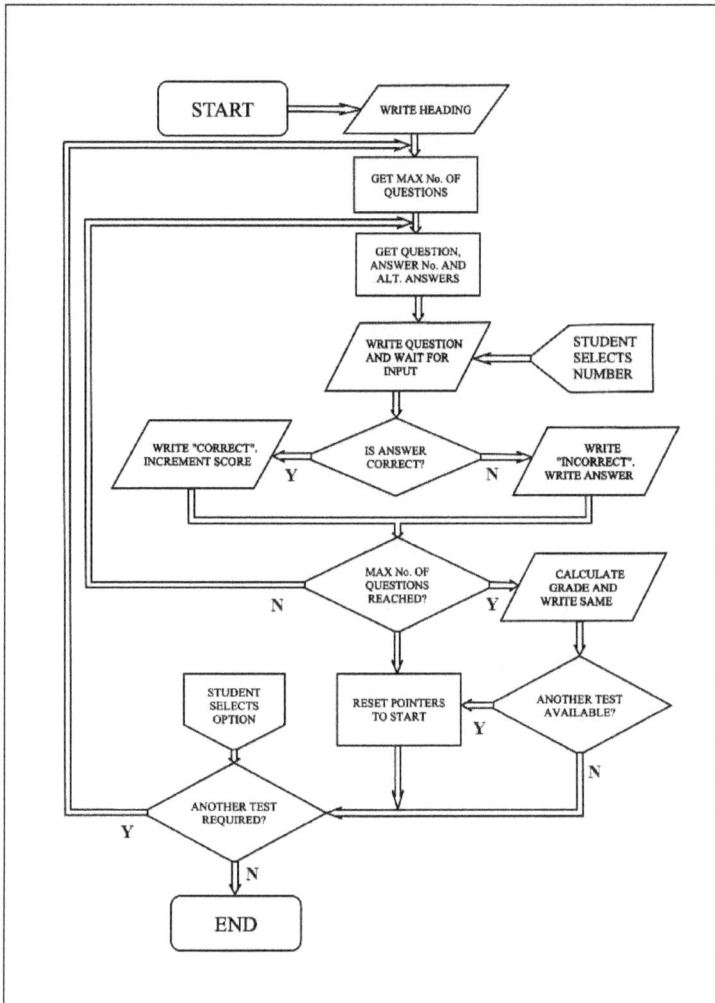

Fig. 6. Typical algorithm of a multiple-choice quiz

The decision-making and branching facility offered by a computer makes it an ideal tool for conducting quizzes, spelling bees and guessing games (e.g. 'Hangman'), but more advanced parsing also enables quite complicated linguistic drills to be simulated with astonishing accuracy. Although not always in fashion, drilling can be an effective technique in modern language teaching and consists mainly of the re-iteration of previously learned structures until they become second nature. In this sense, the term 'train' and 'training' is also used, implying the development of a habitual skill rather than the acquisition of knowledge. It seems to me that the home computer is ideally suited to this kind of work, but it is an area of language activity almost entirely overlooked by software developers. Training or drilling can, indeed must, be repetitive and in order to be effective also requires adequate monitoring, reinforcement and feedback. All of these can be supplied by a normal home computer. The success of drilling depends on many things, on the number of repetitions, their frequency, the relevance of the drills to previously learned material and the nature of the reward or reinforcement when a drill is completed successfully. Essentially a behaviourist device, its classroom use is limited, in practice, to short sessions designed to provide a change of activity from other learning processes. A computer can in such a case take over the role of the teacher, although it is in one sense not teaching but checking. Thus the algorithm of a drilling program is essentially the same as that of a quiz program; the difference lies in the programmer's intention: to reinforce a linguistic structure by repetition rather than to check knowledge through constant quizzing. It is assumed at the outset that the learner will provide the correct response in most cases. The idea is to improve speed and fluency. The computer is not searching for gaps in the learner's knowledge, but is seeking to provide stimulus for controlled repetition of material that has already been learned.

Computer-generated Language Output

From a learner's point of view, one of the most difficult of all English structures is the question tag. The simplicity of the comparable structure in other European languages (e.g. 'nicht wahr?' in German and 'n'est-ce pas?' in French), often results in first language interference and an inability to even accept the need for such a variety of forms as English possesses, let alone learn them. And yet this seemingly insurmountable problem for the learner could not be more suited to the computer, because the structure itself obeys very strict rules of grammar and syntax and morphology which is easy meat for the computer. As far as I know, no question-tag trainer exists for PCs, so I have written the following routine to demonstrate my point:

```pascal
program tags;
        { Question tag tutor by M.Claypole 1989.      }
        { Source code written in Turbo Pascal 5.0 for }
        { IBM PC and compatibles.                     }
        { Compiled version runs under MS-DOS 3.11.    }

uses crt, printer; { screen display and printer   }
                   { control units. May be removed }
                   { if screen control/printer     }
                   { functions are not required    }

type
      WordList = record
                      LexicalItem : string[10];
                      ItemCode    : byte;
                      end;
const
      ProgName    = 'TAGS';
      ProgVers    = '1.6';
      ProgDate    = '17.09.89';
      Author      = 'Maurice Claypole';
      Yes   = 1;
      No    = 0;

      Prompt      = 'Complete with a question tag:';
      VerbFile    = 'VerbFile.dat';
```

```
        PronounFile   = 'PronounFile.dat';

        FirstPerson   =   1;      {    attributes   }
        ThirdPerson   =   2;      {   of lexical    }
        SecondPerson  =   3;      {     items       }
        AuxVerb       =   8;      {    stored       }
        FullVerb      =  16;      {   in single     }
        Present       =  32;      {     byte        }
        Past          =  64;      {   attribute     }
        Exception     = 128;      {     code        }

        NumberOfVerbs      =     32;
        NumberOfPronouns   =      8;
        Delimiter          =    '*';  {  escape key  }
                                      {  for student }
var
        VerbCode      : byte;
        SourceVerb    : string[10];  {   max length  }
        SourcePronoun : string[10];  {   of lexical   }
        PronounCode   : byte;        {     item 10    }
        QuestionTag   : string;
        TargetVerb    : string;
        Tense         : byte;
        Verb          : WordList;
        Pronoun       : WordList,
        DataFile      : text;
        Statement     : string;
        StudentInput  : string;
        Counter       : byte;
        RandomNumber  : byte;
        Score         : byte;
        Attempt       : byte;
        VerbList      : array [1..NumberOfVerbs]of WordList;
        PronounList   : array [1..NumberOfPronouns]of WordList;

function CheckCode(Code:byte):byte; begin
            if (VerbCode and Code)=Code then CheckCode:=Yes else
               CheckCode:=No;
        end;

procedure Evaluate(Input:string);
        begin
            if Input = QuestionTag then
                begin
                   inc(Score);
                   writeln('Correct.'};
                end
            else
                begin
                   if StudentInput = Delimiter then
                      Dec(Attempt)
```

```
                    else
                      write('Incorrect. ');
                        writeln('Correct answer is: ',QuestionTag);
                  end;
            end;

procedure Quiz;
      begin
        writeln(Prompt);
          writeln;
            write(statement,'...');
            readln(StudentInput);
            Evaluate(StudentInput);
          writeln('Score is ',Score , out of ',Attempt);
      end;

procedure GenerateRandomNumber(Range:byte);
      begin
        RandomNumber:=Random(Range) +1;
      end;

procedure EvaluatePronoun;

          {  Development aid only. Routine may  }
          {     be deleted from final version.  }

        begin
          write ('Pronoun   = ',SourcePronoun);
          write ('Pron-Code = ',PronounCode,'      ');

            if (PronounCode and 1) = 1 then write ('1st Pers.');
            if (PronounCode and 2) = 2 then write ('3rd Pers.');
            if (PronounCode and 4) = 4 then write ('2nd/plural');
          writeln;
        end;

procedure ProcessAuxVerb;
      begin
          TargetVerb :=SourceVerb;
      end;

procedure ProcessFullVerb;
      begin
            if CheckCode(Past)=Yes then
              begin
                Tense:=Past;
                TargetVerb:='did';
              end;

            if CheckCode(Present) = Yes then
              begin
                Tense:=Present;
                  if CheckCode(ThirdPerson) =Yes then
```

```
                    begin
                      TargetVerb:='does'
                    end
                  else
                    begin
                     TargetVerb:= 'do';
                     end;
                end;
        end;

procedure EvaluateVerb;

        {  Development aid only. Routine may  }
        {    be deleted from final version.   }

        begin GoToXY(1,2);
                write ('Verb =',SourceVerb);
             GoToXY(20,2);
                write ('Code =',VerbCode);
            GoToXY(35,2);
                if CheckCode(FirstPerson)   = Yes then write('I, ');
                if CheckCode(ThirdPerson)   = Yes then write('he, ');
                if CheckCode(SecondPerson)  = Yes then write('you, ');
                if CheckCode(AuxVerb)       = Yes then write('aux, ');
                if CheckCode(FullVerb)      = Yes then write('full, ');
                if CheckCode(Present)       = Yes then write('present');
                if CheckCode(Past)          = Yes then write('past');
                if CheckCode(Exception)     = Yes then write('exception');
        end;

procedure ProcessVerb;
        begin
            if CheckCode(AuxVerb) = Yes then
                ProcessAuxVerb
            else
                ProcessFullVerb;
        end;

procedure Open{FileName:string);
        begin
            assign(DataFile,FileName);
            reset(DataFile};
        end;

procedure GetPronoun;
        begin
          GenerateRandomNumber(NumberOfPronouns);
          SourcePronoun:=PronounList[RandomNumber].LexicalItem;
          PronounCode:=PronounList[RandomNumber].ItemCode;
        end;

procedure MakePronounArray;

        begin Open(PronounFile};
```

```
            Counter :=1;
              while counter <= numberOfPronouns do
                begin
                  readln(DataFile,Pronoun.LexicalItem};
                  readln(DataFile,Pronoun.ItemCode};
                      PronounList[Counter].LexicalItem:=Pronoun.LexcalItem;
                      PronounList[Counter].itemCode:=Pronoun.ItemCode;
                  inc(Counter};
                  end;
            Close(DataFile};
            Counter:=0;
      end;

procedure ReadVerbFile;
      begin
          Counter :=1;
          GenerateRandomNumber(NumberOfVerbs);
          while Counter < RandomNumber do
              begin
                readln(DataFile,Verb.LexicalItem};
                readln{DataFile,Verb.ItemCode};
                inc(Counter);
              end;
            Counter:=0;
      end;

procedure GetVerb;

      begin
        repeat
          GenerateRandomNumber(NumberOfVerbs};
          SourceVerb:=VerbList[RandomNumber].LexicalItem;
          VerbCode:=VerbList[RandomNumber].ItemCode;
        until (VerbCode and PronounCode}=PronounCode;
      end;

procedure MakeVerbArray;
      begin
        Open (verbfile);
        Counter:=1;
        while Counter <= NumberOfVerbs do
          begin Readln(DataFile,Verb.LexicalItem);
            Readln(DataFile,Verb.ItemCode);
            VerbList[Counter].LexicalItem:=Verb.LexicalItem;
            VerbList[Counter].ItemCode:=Verb.ItemCode;
            Inc(Counter);
          end;
        Close (DataFile) ;
      end;

procedure Heading;
      begin
        ClrScr;
          write(ProgName,' by ',Author);
```

```
            writeln(' Vers. ',ProgVers,' of ',ProgDate);
            writeln;
      end;

procedure Instructions;
      {  Here the user interface language is English  }
      {    but instructions could be given be in the   }
      {       learner's native language, if known.      }

      begin
        writeln('This program is intended to provide practice in');
        writeln('forming question tags.');
        writeln;
        writeln('The computer will ask you to complete a random');
        writeln('selection of sentences by adding an appropriate');
        writeln('question tag. You may attempt up to 254 problems');
        writeln('at each sitting, but have only one guess at each.');
        writeln('The computer will automatically show your score.');
        writeln('When you have had enough practice, just hit the');
        writeln('"',Delimiter, '" key.');
        writeln;
        writeln('Remember to complete each question tag with a');
        writeln('question mark, and to hit the RETURN key when');
        writeln('you have typed in your answer.');
        writeln;
      end;

procedure CheckException;
      begin
        if CheckCode(Exception) = Yes then
          begin
            if SourceVerb = 'am' then TargetVerb   := 'are';
            if SourceVerb = 'can' then TargetVerb  := 'ca';
            if SourceVerb = 'will' then TargetVerb := 'wo';
          end;
      end;

procedure MakeStatement;
      begin
          Statement:=SourcePronoun+' '+SourceVerb+', ';
      end;

procedure MakeQuestionTag;
      begin
        TargetVerb := TargetVerb+'n"t';
        QuestionTag:= TargetVerb + ' '+ SourcePronoun+'?';
      end;

procedure Escape;
      begin
        writeln;
        writeln('You have had 254 attempts. That is the');
        writeln('end of this session. Hit the RETURN key');
```

```
        writeln('to end the program. Thank you for being');
        writeln('so diligent.');
        readln;
     end;

begin {main program}
        Attempt        := 1;
        Score          := 0;
        Student Input  := ' ';
        Heading;
        Instructions;
        Randomize;
        MakePronounArray;
        MakeVerbArray;

        while StudentInput <> Delimiter do
           begin
             Counter:=0;
              GetPronoun;
               GetVerb;
                ProcessVerb:
                 MakeStatement;
                  CheckException;
                   MakeQuestionTag;
                   Quiz:
                     Inc(Attempt);
                      if Attempt >= 255 then
                         begin
                            Escape;
                            exit;
                         end;
end;
```

This demonstration routine is not intended to offer the ultimate in student-computer interaction, merely to demonstrate how a relatively simple software routine can process NL problems on the basis of a Boolean grammatical truth table rather than by means of semantic concordance. In other words, the program does not merely produce output based on static data stored in RAM but actually generates dynamic output according to a specific set of grammatical principles and exceptions.

The routine could easily be adapted to create a more interactive student-machine dialogue if student-formed statements were to be checked against the verb and subject database for concordance and the resultant attribute codes then used to generate the correct question tag. This would provide the student with a useful problem-solving tool.

The contents of the data files accompanying the TAGS program are coded according to the function of each lexical item. The binary scheme shown below was used to store the attributes of each lexical item as a single byte and enable the program routines to identify the type of pronouns and verbs and to match these with each other and to determine whether an auxiliary verb would be needed in forming a question tag, and if so, in which sense this should be. Furthermore, the anomalies by which 'can' + 'n't' is contracted to 'can't', 'will' + 'n't' becomes 'won't' and the question tag to 'r am' is transformed into 'aren't I' had to be identified parsing for an additional exception check code bit (the MSB in the table below).

The table below shows the lexical items used in an initial test run together with their decimal and binary codes. The verb list represents a random selection in no particular sequence. Any list of verbs in the present and preterite tenses may be used. It is merely necessary to amend the appropriate variables in the source code of the program. For the purposes of this demonstration, the verb 'have' was treated as an auxiliary verb only. The program can be expanded to encompass a wider variety of grammatical subjects, hence the decision to store pronoun data as a file rather than as program variables. The addition of random or selective predicates (coded, for example, by adding a second attribute byte) would further enhance the usefulness of the program.

The attribute codes include an element of redundancy and could easily be streamlined to increase the number of attributes per bit. The bit pattern of the lexical item attribute byte for verbs is as follows:

Decimal	Binary	Attribute
	MSB LSB	
1	00000001	first person
2	00000010	third person
4	00000100	second person/plural
8	00001000	auxiliary verb
16	00010000	full verb
32	00100000	present tense
64	01000000	preterite
128	10000000	exception

Thus, a random selection of verbs would have a truth table like this:

Bit	8	7	6	5	4	3	2	1
Att	exc	pret	pres	full	aux	2nd	3rd	1st
Dec	128	64	32	16	8	4	2	1
am	169	1	0	1	0	1	0	0	1
are	48	0	0	1	0	1	1	0	0
is	42	0	0	1	0	1	0	1	0
will	175	1	0	1	0	1	1	1	1
could	75	0	1	0	0	1	1	1	1
can	175	1	0	1	0	1	1	1	1
had	79	0	1	0	0	1	1	1	1
have	45	0	0	1	0	1	1	0	1
has	42	0	0	1	0	1	0	1	0
go	53	0	0	1	1	0	1	0	1
goes	50	0	0	1	1	0	0	1	0
went	87	0	1	0	1	0	1	1	1
eat	53	0	0	1	1	0	1	0	1
like	53	0	0	1	1	0	1	0	1

likes	50	0	0	1	1	0	0	1	0
ate	87	0	1	0	1	0	1	1	1
sing	53	0	0	1	1	0	1	0	1
sang	87	0	1	0	0	0	1	1	1
bring	53	0	0	1	1	0	1	0	1
brought	87	0	1	0	1	0	1	1	1
brings	50	0	0	1	1	0	0	1	0
catch	53	0	0	1	1	0	1	0	1
caught	87	0	1	0	1	0	1	1	1
catches	50	0	0	1	1	0	0	1	0
find	53	0	0	1	1	0	1	0	1
found	87	0	1	0	1	0	1	1	1
finds	50	0	0	1	1	0	0	1	0
love	53	0	0	1	1	0	1	0	1
loves	50	0	0	1	1	0	0	1	0
loved	87	0	1	0	1	0	1	1	1
must	47	0	0	1	0	1	1	1	1
should	47	0	0	1	0	1	1	1	1

The pronouns follow a corresponding scheme, but utilize only the three least significant bits:

Bit		8	7	6	5	4	3	2	1
Att		-------		unused		-------	3rd	2nd	1st
Dec		128	64	32	16	8	4	2	1
I	1	0	0	0	0	0	0	0	1
he	2	0	0	0	0	0	0	1	0
she	2	0	0	0	0	0	0	1	0
it	2	0	0	0	0	0	0	1	0
one	2	0	0	0	0	0	0	1	0
we	4	0	0	0	0	0	1	0	0
you	4	0	0	0	0	0	1	0	0
they	4	0	0	0	0	0	1	0	0

Software Development Systems

Although CALL systems are widespread in some countries (USA, Japan, England), they are relatively under-developed in Germany. Often, the computer is disregarded as useless in this respect because it does not speak. Reference has already been made to the inadequacies of available speech digitisers, and it must be borne in mind that other self-study techniques (audio cassettes, Superlearning, direct broadcasting) are available and are to some extent in direct competition with software products. Even such speech digitisers as are available provide no model for pronunciation and in any case there are currently no language teaching programs available which exploit the speech capability of microcomputers. Single-purpose devices are available (hand-held spelling checkers and vocabulary trainers) but these are so primitive as to be disregarded.

The majority of programs currently available merely compare the student's input with the predetermined answers and are therefore dependent on direct parsing and the knowledge and ability of the software engineer. Ideally, of course, the programmer should also be an experienced teacher or educationalist and aware of the many traps that direct concordance language parsing entails. Sadly, this is often not the case. Much also depends on whether or not a dedicated authoring system is used. A good example of an authoring system available for language training using a PC is a series of programming tools by the British teacher and programmer Christopher Jones. Two of these, *Gapmaster* and *Matchmaster*, are described below.

Gapmaster

This is an authoring system used for producing conventional cloze-type completion exercises. The gap to be completed by the student can be up to 150 characters long and, within this constraint, can contain any number of words. A variety of correct answers can be accepted, and each gap can be supported by help routines. In addition, provision is made for the creation of full-screen help pages. The teacher or developer coding an application for use by autonomous learners therefore has a fair amount of scope and flexibility to develop useful and meaningful training exercises. For the student, this means that they can make use of a variety of help-functions and hints whilst trying to complete the gaps. Function keys may also be used to ascertain the length of the anticipated answer and/or the number of words it contains. The system responds to the student's input by advising them that a given input is right or wrong, too long or too short. At the end of each exercise, an evaluation of the student's performance is displayed in percentage terms, together with the suggestion that the exercise should be repeated if less than 90 % was achieved. Any teacher wishing to adapt the resultant material to a classroom situation or any independent learners with only sporadic access to a computer can print out the cloze exercises so that they can be filled in on paper, which, however, sacrifices the help routines which are an integral part of the teaching system.

Matchmaster

This tool is used to write allocation exercises in which pairs, for example German and English vocabulary items or the beginning and end of sentences, are compared with each other Each half of a matchable pair can contain up to 120 characters. A help screen can be provided, and a hard copy can be printed out for classroom or offline use. The student can call up the help page or can demand the answer. The system responds simply with 'right' or 'wrong' or 'you tried that already'. A tally is kept of the points scored and the totals are displayed at the end of the exercise in the following manner:

1. Total number of pairs

2. Total number of pairs correct

3. Total number of errors

4. Total number of pairs attempted

5. Result as a percentage

Here too, a score of less than 90 % results in the student being asked to take the test again.

Extensions of the pair-matching system are a Memory game and a game similar to Snap, in which the student's speed of response is tested.

An interesting development in the field of CAESP (and an exception to the rule that CAESP differs from CAEFL only in its knowledge base) is MS Management Simulation by WDK Sprachen and ISE Daten.

This is a management game which can be implemented by a teacher or instructor in English or German as an exercise in communication or for foreign language training purposes. The basic idea is based on the following scenario: A company is taken over and run by a new management team (the students). Various companies are in competition in the market area selected. The management must make decisions based on the following criteria: selling price, marketing, production figures, company management, production capacity, dividends, taking of credits, selling of shares, investment in other companies. This is done after first establishing the company policy, its goals and strategies. In addition, quarterly results must be analysed, and the students' analysis and decisions are fed into the computer. The success of each company therefore depends on the computer's analysis of the students' own inputs and on the decisions and inputs of the competitors. The program runs on IBM PCs and compatibles under MS-DOS and PC-DOS.

Programming Languages

The most widely used high-level programming language available for PCs and HCs is BASIC, which in its various dialects has become the standard 'beginner's' language whilst retaining a degree of flexibility which makes it suitable for handling logical, mathematical and textual problems. A simple BASIC CALL routine (Telling the Time in German) has already been discussed and is reproduced in Appendix I. BASIC is, however, largely unstructured and if handled carelessly can lack transparency. In addition, many dialects offer somewhat limited instruction sets and inadequate string handling. When dealing with complicated linguistic structures, the CALL designer would be well advised to look elsewhere for software tools. It is therefore useful in this context to briefly review some of the other programming languages currently available for microcomputers. Considering the wealth of languages and dialects currently available, I make no claim to completeness and have consciously omitted such languages as FORTRAN, ALGOL and COBOL, which have only minority or specialized applications outside the scope of language learning and consequently have no relevance here.

LOGO

One of the most exciting developments in programming languages was the attempt by Seymour Papert (1980) to develop an interactive child-oriented programming language. Concepts such as turtle graphics, using relative screen positions in addition to absolute ones, make this an excellent language for children to learn. The language is designed to increase the child's ability for self-expression and improve communicative powers both during computer dialog (logic training and clear expression) and, by extension, in human interaction.

LOGO uses keywords (DRAW, PENUP, FORWARD) which are somewhat closer to the user's own language than the majority of high-level languages and is one of the few programming languages to be available in different human-language variants. Thus, a German version of LOGO uses German keywords rather than English ones. Furthermore, unlike BASIC, LOGO offers the user the opportunity to expand his or her 'vocabulary' by constructing named subroutines which can then be incorporated into subsequent programs. Essentially, however, LOGO provides a tool for children to experiment with rather than a software tool for the CALL designer. The following LOGO routine designed to draw a series of graphic 'waves' shows both the similarity to BASIC and the use of relative screen positions not typically available in BASIC:

```
DO WAVE
FOR X = 1 TO 30
FORWARD 10, LEFT X
NEXT X
END

PLACE 100,20
WAVE
```

```
PLACE  40,20
TURN  0
WAVE
PLACE  160,20
TURN  0
WAVE
```

On a 300 x 200 pixel screen, this simple routine produces the image shown in Fig. 7.

Fig. 7. Screen output of LOGO 'waves' program

Forth

Forth was originally designed as a control language for machine tools and similar industrial purposes but because it is based on the concept of the stack and the vocabulary, it has also been used to design electronic dictionaries and has applications beyond its designers' original intentions. In Forth, new 'words' can easily be defined during programming, or new meanings can be assigned to existing ones.

The definitions (functions) are, in effect, entered direct from the keyboard to the stack and can be pulled off the stack only in reverse order. It is therefore critical to know which element is at the TOS (top of stack) at any given time. Since the user (i.e. the programmer) can construct his own definitions, the scope for invention is virtually unlimited, but programs can very quickly become indecipherable. The 'dictionary' concept makes it an ideal language for storing linguistic equivalents, as, for example, in a translation program. In Forth, assignations are made by using a colon followed by the word to be defined, followed by an expression or statement (which may include previously defined keywords or expressions or statements). In the pre-defined instruction set, a full stop is used to pull words from the stack (which has the effect of generating output) and a space is used as a delimiter between expressions. The end of a definition is indicated by a semi-colon. Thus the following line

```
: TABLE ." TISCH" ;
```

assigns the German word 'TISCH' to the English word 'TABLE'. From now on, 'table' will be read and printed (i.e. pulled off the stack) as 'Tisch'.

Forth is available for most HC and PC versions but, perhaps because of its apparent complexity and unfamiliar structure (using for example inverted Polish notation), is not in widespread use. Furthermore, it is not a convenient tool for handling large items of text-based data. Its applications for CALL purposes are therefore somewhat limited.

PILOT

As a programming language, PILOT actually predates LOGO but is worthy of attention here as it was designed as a tool for the communicative knowledge to others, i.e. in contrast to LOGO, it is a language for teachers rather than learners. It is relatively easy to construct simple question and answer routines and enhance them with graphics and sound. A PILOT program consists essentially of lines of command words (each consisting of one or two letters) followed by their arguments. In the following example, the traditional Nimo matchstick game, the keyword 'T' (for 'Text') generates output to the screen. 'A', 'M', 'N' and 'Y' are used to get input from the user and to compare them with predefined alternatives.

```
R:21 MATCHSTICKS
T:WHAT'S YOUR NAME?
?:
T:HI ?$,WE TAKE TURNS AT REMOVING MATCHES
T:FROM THE TABLE. WE CAN TAKE 1,2 OR 3 MATCHES
T:AT A TIME. WHOEVER TAKES THE LAST MATCH LOSES.
*SC:A=21
C:B=21
*HT:
T:YOUR GO:
I:CC:D=4-C
T:1 TAKE $D
C:A=A-4
C:B=B-4
T:NEW TOTAL IS $A
C:$=B
M:101
NY:H
T:YOU NOW HAVE TO TAKE THE LAST MATCH,SO I WIN.
T:DO YOU WANT ANOTHER GO?
A:
M:Y,YES
YS:S
T:DON'T GET MAD. I ALWAYS WIN!
S:
```

Since the instruction set is based on the question and answer session, it is apparent that language drills and vocabulary tests require much less programming effort in PILOT than in many other languages. PILOT is, however, not readily available for the majority of home computers and seems to have been largely ignored by software developers.

ELAN

Unlike the other programming languages mentioned, ELAN was developed in Germany. The syntax is similar in structure to ALGOL or Pascal. ELAN, however, also offers 'refinements', which make it possible to incorporate names and terms in a program even though they may not be defined until later. ELAN is therefore suitable for a top-down approach in which the programmer first organizes the task in general terms and refines it as work progresses. A task is broken down into software modules which may be called from another program without the programmer being concerned about the internal structure of existing modules. First of all, routines are declared/called, and are subsequently defined in detail as refinements. A definition is introduced by an end-of-line colon. A typical example is given below.

```
PRIMENUMBERS:
   BEGIN TABLE;
   WHILE
   Z<1000
   REP
      TEST WHETHER Z IS A PRIME;
      TEST
      NEXT NUMBER
   ENDREP.
BEGIN TABLE:
      PUT ("PRIMES BELOW 1000");
      LINE(1);
      PUT(2);
      INT VAR Z::3.
```

```
TEST WHETHER Z IS A PRIME:
    INT VAR A::3;
    WHILE
        Z COULD BE DIVISIBLE
    REP
      TRY TO DIVIDE BY A
      INCREMENT A
    ENDREP:
    PUT(Z).
Z COULD BE DIVISIBLE BY 2:
    A * A <= Z.
TRY TO DIVIDE BY A:
    IF (Z MOD A) = THEN LEAVE TRY TO DIVIDE BY A
    FI.
    INCREMENT Z:
    A INCR 2.
TEST NEXT NUMBER:
    Z INCR 2.
```

This top-down approach makes ELAN a useful vehicle for experimentation and the language is in use in a number of German schools and universities. However, it is only readily available for the EUMEL operating system such as used by the Olivetti M20, and not for MS-DOS or any other common PC operating systems.

Pascal

Next to BASIC, Pascal is one of the most widely used programming languages in schools and universities and Pascal compilers are readily available in a variety of versions for most PCs. There are even compiler versions available for interpreter-oriented HCs such as the Commodore 64 and 128. The latter, however, tend to be hybrids, using the BASIC interpreter (complete with line numbers) and extending its scope by the addition of Pascal keywords, so that both BASIC and Pascal code can be written. This brings added advantages, but also the disadvantage of making a once structured language unstructured again. In standard Pascal, each variable must be declared before use (either as a local or global variable) and a variety of data types (byte, word, string, text, etc.) are available so the careful selection of the correct data type greatly enhances efficiency during execution. Pascal programs consist of procedures and functions, each of which performs a specific task, and a program rump in which the control sequence for the final execution is declared. More programming discipline is required than with BASIC or ELAN, but the beauty of Pascal lies in its adaptability. It is equally suited as a development tool for mathematical, textual and logical operations. It is therefore a useful programming tool for CALL applications. The Tags program previously discussed presents a working example of a CAEFL program written in Pascal.

C

Although usually associated with the Unix and Xenix operating systems, the programming language C is now readily available in several versions for most PCs.

C offers the programmer a powerful tool for designing efficient routines in a low-level language approaching machine code.

Similar in structure to Pascal, C uses the function as the basic building block of a program. As with Pascal, the functions are declared first and then followed by a rump (in C this is the function 'main()' which causes the code to be executed. However, the syntax of C makes it an overly complex language to work with for anyone except an enthusiast, as the following example shows:

```
main ()
{
    int birth_yr, cur_ry;
```

```
printf("Enter year of birth: ");
scanf("%d",&birth_yr);
if(birth_yr <=0)
    printf(" Invalid year\n");
printf("Enter current year: ");
scanf ("%d", &cur_yr);
if(cur_yr<=0)
    printf(" Invalid year\n");
printf(" Your age = %d\n",cur_yr-birth_yr);
}
```

Although Lisp is one of the oldest AI programming languages, it (and its recent offshoot, CLOS – common lisp object system) is the favourite programming language of many developers using larger systems. However, no Lisp versions are currently available for PC or HC operating systems.

New Software Tools

At the time of writing, more advanced SW tools are beginning to appear on the German market which will hopefully revolutionize the teachware available for HC and PC applications. The latest Pascal versions, Turbo Pascal 5.5 (Borland) and Quick Pascal (Microsoft) are languages which to a limited extent at least support object-oriented software development (OOSD) and therefore provide expert system (ES) and knowledge base system (KBS) tools for the PC which bring the goal of a near-NL interface for these machines somewhat nearer. Compared with previous Borland Pascal products, Turbo Pascal 5.5 offers dynamic object-oriented programming together with a much higher compiling speed and a much-improved overlay manager. Also available is a new Turbo Assembler and Debugger (V. 1.5) which further enhance the OOSD functions by providing a means of tracing the hierarchy of objects and investigating the types of objects assigned. Following the introduction of C++ and Object Pascal for the Apple MacIntosh, both of these new Pascal dialects, Turbo Pascal and Quick Pascal are now available for the first time for the IBM-PC and enable the key principles of OOSD techniques to be implemented, namely:

1. Classification of software modules (objects)

2. Inheritance – similarities between objects

3. Polymorphism – variable structure of objects

4. Static objects – corresponding in structure to procedures

5. Dynamic objects – objects which receive their final structure at the execution stage.

Both Turbo Pascal 5.5 and Quick Pascal are supplied as coding environments complete with improved development support functions (Figs. 8 and 9).

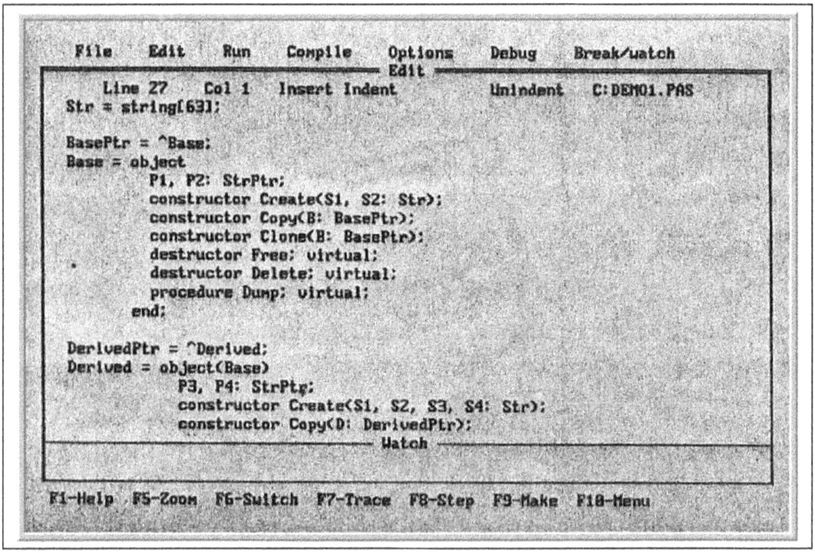

Fig. 8. Coding screens for object-oriented software development under Turbo Pascal 5.5

One of the most significant developments to be expected in the early 1990's is the advent of integrated knowledge base systems for the PC. Although not yet (in the summer of 1989) available on the German market, the American software company Knowledge Garden has announced a series of AI development systems for the PC. Pre-delivery reports indicate that this will consist of an integrated AI programming language and ES dialog interface for hypertext applications. The whole packet has therefore been dubbed 'Hypertextpert'.

The AI programming language, *Knowledgepro* offers a topic-oriented structure of inheritances which can be passed on to subsequent topics. A topic in this sense could be a highlighted section (usually a word) in a hypertext document which, when selected, is executed by the system. The selected topic is not of a fixed structure and may in turn be a section of text or a software routine. Topics may be nested and may recursively call topics higher in the hierarchy. Clearly, there are parallels to be drawn to our previous discussion of objects in relation to Turbo Pascal 5 and Quick Pascal. The essential difference lies in the applications environment of *Knowledgepro*, taken together with the *Textpro* hypertext document generating system and another program from the same stable, *Knowledgemaker*, which can be used to inductively create the rules for a knowledge base.

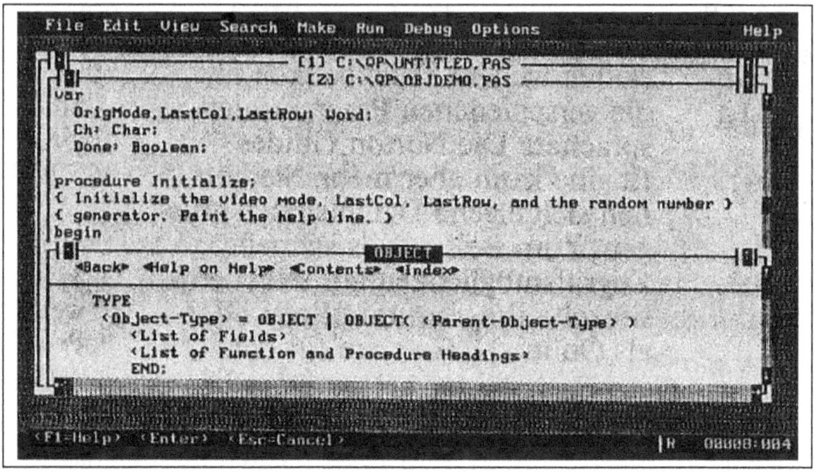

Fig. 9. Coding screen for object-oriented software development
under Quick Pascal

These rules can then be implemented either in a *Knowledgepro* program or in Turbo Prolog or indeed in any other ES shell available for the PC. See Fig. 10.

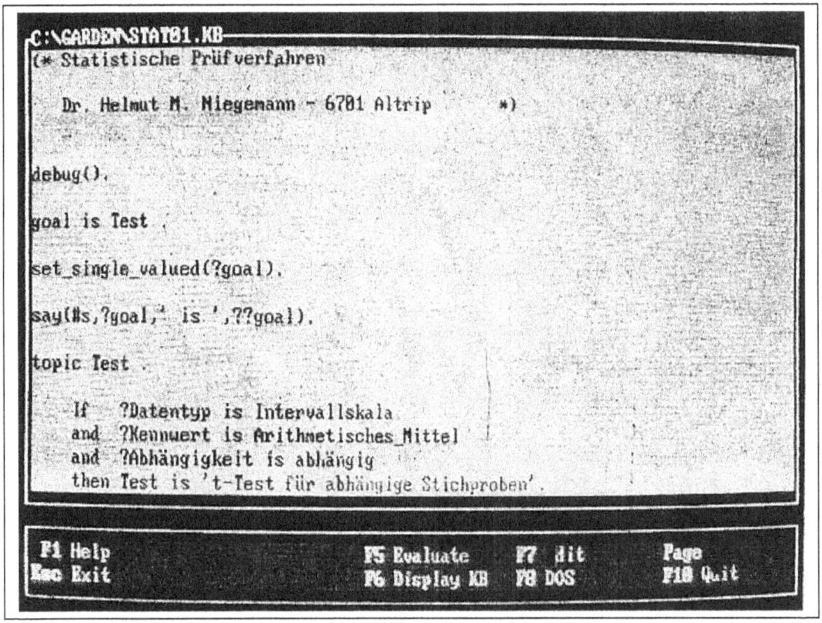

```
C:\GARDEN\STAT01.KB
(* Statistische Prüfverfahren

   Dr. Helmut M. Niegemann - 6701 Altrip        *)


debug().

goal is Test .

set_single_valued(?goal).

say(#s,?goal, is ',??goal).

topic Test .

   If   ?Datentyp is Intervallskala
   and  ?Kennwert is Arithmetisches_Mittel
   and  ?Abhängigkeit is abhängig
   then Test is 't-Test für abhängige Stichproben'.
```

| F1 Help | | F5 Evaluate | F7 Edit | Page |
| Esc Exit | | F6 Display KB | F8 DOS | F10 Quit |

Fig. 10. Program code of a Knowledgepro application showing syntax
and structure

In line with the software paradigm shift I referred to in the introduction, some development systems previously only available for larger systems are being offered the PC, in some cases with severe restrictions. Thus, Smalltalk 80, currently the most widespread object-oriented programming language outside the world of the PC, is now for the first time available for a number of PCs including Apple Macintosh, HP 9000, Atari and

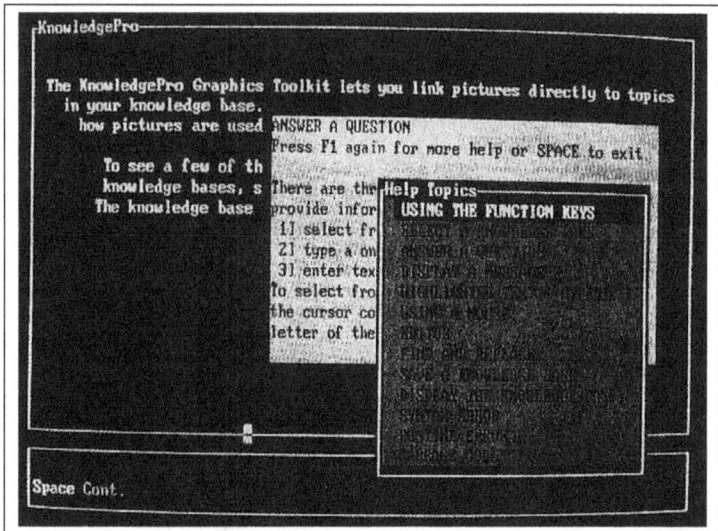

Fig. 11. Knowledgepro development environment

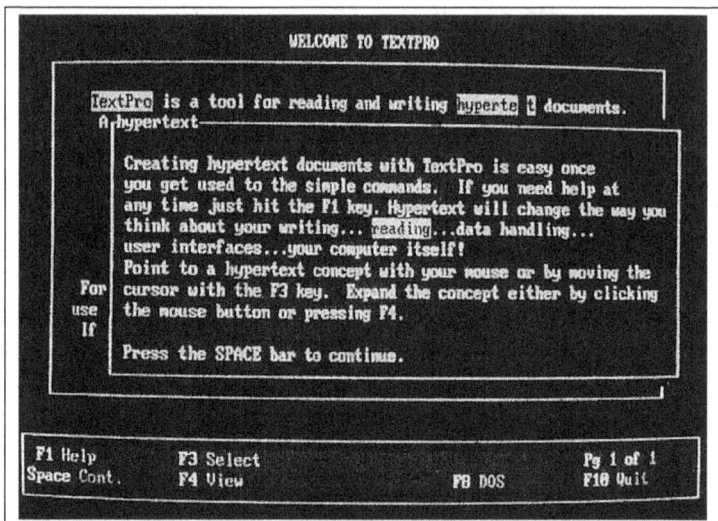

Fig. 12. Knowledgepro hypertext application

the IBM-PC. The requirements of the MS-DOS version, however, preclude its implementation on the majority of PCs currently in use. The only PC version of this language is Smalltalk 80 Version 2.4 from ParcPlace, and this runs only on machines based on the more powerful Intel 80386 32-bit CPU, whereas most machines currently in use incorporate the 8086 (8-bit) processor and the majority of new hardware coming onto the market is limited to the 80286 (16-bit) chip. Furthermore, a minimum of 3 MB of random access memory are required, whereas most PCs offer a maximum of the 640 KB accessible via the standard MS-DOS operating system. The development environment can only be used at the upper end of the PC spectrum. An interface to the programming language C is provided, but only one C compiler (Metaware C) was supported by the version under test. The windows technology and the incorporated system browser facilitate the definition of new classes and the analysis of existing hierarchies.

A Smalltalk program consists of a collection of Classes for which various Methods are defined and is executed by sending a message to a previously defined START Class, e.g.

```
PROJECT START
```

This class therefore corresponds to the program rump of a Pascal program or the 'Main{}' function of a C program. Although Smalltalk variables must be declared before use, they are not assigned to types until the program is executed. Thus, the variable type declarations of, for example, Pascal, are super-fluous, making the development of a Smalltalk application less tiresome and more flexible. Numerical variables can be declared and assigned in the following form:

```
| a b |
a:=100
b:=a*a.
```

In Smalltalk, each expression represents a message which has been sent to an object (a class or an instance of a class). Thus the expression 'a:=100' above (already instantly recognizable to the Pascal programmer) in effect means that the message ':=' is sent to the object 'a' with the parameter '100', causing the value '100' to be assigned to 'a'. Thus the standard syntax of a Smalltalk expression is

```
recipient message parameter
```

Expressions may be enclosed in square brackets to form blocks (corresponding to 'BEGIN ... END' in Pascal or { and } in C):

```
['Disk Drive not ready!' Display].
```

Such blocks may themselves be treated as objects. They can be passed on as parameters and acted upon by the recipient of a message, as in the following example:

```
ChkDrive Test Error:
['Disk Drive not ready!' Display].
```

These block arguments are themselves objects and can therefore also receive messages. Control structures (e.g. loops) utilize the block structure:

```
[input atEnd] whileFalse:
[output nextPut: input next].
```

This fragment therefore copies the file named 'input' to the file named 'output'.

Once tools such as those discussed have been implemented in the PC area with a view to producing convincing ML-NL interfaces for CAEFL purposes, the greatest single obstacle to their successful implementation in this area is likely to be the nature of the KB, since the hardware limitations of the present generation of PCs preclude the storage of sufficient knowledge to maintain a sustained dialog outside a limited subject area. The goal in this context, however, is not to pass the Turing test (see Part Two) nor to give the user the impression that they are in dialog with a human, but is a much more modest one, that of providing a useful tool for practicing a foreign language in limited situations, and there is no reason why programs should not soon be designed in which the machine simulates (for the purposes of language practice) a waiter or a customs officer engaging the student in foreign language dialog and providing assistance in problem areas without the function of the machine being reduced to that of an electronic reference book or programmed learning text.

The problem is therefore one of software design, and in this connection it is useful to look at software development in the wider context of human language interaction and artificial intelligence. Consequently, in Part Two, I cast my net beyond the limitations of existing user systems and the easily accessible microcomputers of today in order to deal with some of the theoretical implications and furthermore, to point towards possible developments for the future.

PART TWO

CAEFL and Artificial Intelligence

Introduction

The frustration experienced by many users of language learning programs and the barriers that I have encountered in my search for a useful teaching tool has led me to investigate precisely why there are no really useful systems available for the autonomous language learner. This in turn leads to the need to understand the fundamental differences between human and computer 'intelligence'. A detailed study of the state of the art of artificial intelligence systems is therefore called for. And if we are to postulate the development of automated systems that can take on the role of language teacher, we need to consider both monolingual and bilingual teaching environments. Clearly, the ability to navigate a single language efficiently is a prerequisite for the ability to operate in two languages simultaneously, as a foreign-language teacher working in a monolingual environment often needs to.

Crucial to the flow of natural language and to human linguistic interchange is knowledge of the real world, and one of the major difficulties in programming computers to interact with humans is that of providing the computer with adequate knowledge of the world in order to give the appearance of understanding or to make an actual interpretive leap of the kind which humans take for granted. Such 'communicative competence' (Higgins & Johns, 1984) normally extends beyond the boundaries of a single sentence and is largely beyond the scope of current CALL systems, which concentrate on 'linguistic competence', i.e. linguistic structural correctness. That linguistic correctness and communicative correctness are not always the same can be demonstrated by the expression

You ain't seen nothing yet

In parsing this input, a computer application embodying only linguistic recognition capabilities would (assuming it could cope with the variant *ain't* in the first place) recognize the double negative as cancelling itself out and assume that the message was equivalent to

> *You have already seen something*

whereas the real (communicative) meaning is closer to

> *There's more where that came from.*

Expert Systems and AI

As early as 1950, Alan Turing had suggested that the only test of whether a machine was intelligent or not should be an operational one. If someone could communicate with a computer in a natural language in such a way that they could not distinguish between its responses and those of a human operator, the test would be deemed to have been passed. One response to this was Weizenbaum's Eliza, an algorithm capable of being supplied with different scenarios. Such an artificial and obviously simulated dialog quickly fails to pass the test but may provide an interesting linguistic interchange through simple parsing of the user's input.

Although the Turing Test is often used as a kind of ultimate determiner in the field of Artificial Intelligence, it is my view that the test itself is far from well conceived. For educational purposes, an inability to distinguish between a human and a machine is not necessarily desirable, and in the context of modern expert systems, it is a potential hazard.

Let us assume, for instance, that during a Turing trial, I ask the same question ten times and receive ten identical answers from one source whilst the other source of answers produces different responses which are indicative of inconsistency, boredom and sheer contrariness. I will immediately identify the latter source as a human. It would, however, not be in the interests of an engineer, a pilot or a CAEFL student to receive conflicting 'human' responses on the basis of the respondent's whims. Human traits may be easily identifiable, but this does not mean that they are desirable in a machine or in an expert system.

Let us take this idea further and assume that the response to a technical query is, 'I did know what the value was, but I have forgotten'. From a human, we would accept this; if it came from a computer we would be very angry indeed. This also brings into question the very notion of 'intelligence'. Because the current state of AI systems is fairly primitive, we assume that humans are more intelligent, but we often identify humans by those traits (forgetfulness, inconsistency) which manifestly demonstrate an inefficient form of information processing when compared to the machine. If, during a Turing trial, we identify a human on the basis of forgetfulness, we declare the machine to have failed the intelligence test, whereas in actual fact it has demonstrated a precision and consistency of which its human competitor has not been capable. We may argue, of course, that originality and imagination are of a higher order of intelligence than information processing, but it is questionable whether this type of non-quantifiable intelligence is a requirement for a given expert system application.

An important milestone in the development of AI was reached by Winograd with SHRDLU, in which a computer was programmed with reasonably complete information about a limited world consisting of three-dimensional objects of different colours which it could manipulate in response to instructions given in English. In such a limited sphere of activity, it is possible for a computer to hold a reasonably convincing dialog with humans in such a way that, indirectly at least, language acquisition might take place. Such programs were the forerunners of the knowledge-based expert systems in use or under development today, in which the computer is not expected to compete with the average human on equal terms with reference to the whole world, but can be programmed with more information than is available to a specific user relating to a clearly defined and contextually limited knowledge environment.

The original conception of the computer as a device to do computation has been surpassed. Today, we must regard the computer as a 'general symbol manipulation device' (Fisher, 1986). The development of heuristic rather than algorithmic programs has resulted in a change of perspective and led to the creation of a number of manipulable symbolic representations systems. The introduction of Lisp by John McCarthy was an important breakthrough in this direction and the work has been carried on through the other programming languages referred to in this book as well as through the development of expert systems and expert system shells.

Furthermore, information processing reaches out beyond the bounds of mere computation when computers are used by humans to assist them in such activities as document production, message transmission and related information processing tasks which require little in the way of actual computation, but demand a flexible and interactive development and editing environment and above all a user-friendly and truly interactive human language/machine language communication interface.

Knowledge-based Systems

I have already discussed some modern dialog game versions, which offer the student the opportunity to take part in heuristic problem-solving situations. The more serious implementation of this technique can be found in the context of the latest knowledge-based systems which use natural language or near-natural language to solve a problem with the aid of, in effect, an electronic slave. The difficulty of handling natural language is, however, exemplified by the inadequacy of state-of-the-art translation programs to achieve even a semblance of sustained and convincing natural language (see my comments on the Siemens METAL program below).

A further requirement of knowledge-based systems and expert systems is knowledge of the real world and although hierarchic development concepts such as OOSD can help us to partially overcome these difficulties, the task of simulating natural language leaves us with a considerable mountain to climb.

The main difficulty involved in coding routines for language teaching purposes is that natural language often does not behave in such a way as to be easily broken down into algorithmic patterns. Margaret Boden (1985) points out that even a naive user of human language constantly makes assumptions about language of which a computer is scarcely capable and might easily overestimate the ability of a computer in a dialog situation if the computer's own vocabulary is limited to such expressions as can be given a fixed meaning or a valence on a strict valuation scheme (e.g. probably, possibly, never). In human terms, however, non-monotonic reasoning often prevails over fixed truth. In non-monotonic reasoning a proposition can change its truth value as knowledge progresses. In other words, learning can take place. This is standard practice in a human environment, but not so in the world of computer-driven intelligence in which knowledge is often assumed to be a fixed quantity. Work is being undertaken in this area, but so far, real success has not been achieved. John McCarthy (1986), one of the main instigators of AI and whom we have already referred to as the creator of the programming language Lisp, uses the example of the cannibal puzzle to demonstrate this:

On one side of a river there are three missionaries and three cannibals and there is one rowing boat which can hold two persons. Assuming that at no time must there be more cannibals than missionaries in any one place, the problem is, how do the missionaries get across the river without any of them being eaten?

Assuming a limited world consisting of only the elements stated in the puzzle, there is little difference between the human approach of taking pencil and paper and trying to work out the solution and an algorithmic computer program. However, if a human wanted to tease the problem setter, they could spontaneously produce an almost infinite number of alternative solutions: the cannibals hire a helicopter, they use a nearby bridge, they build a raft, etc. At each new suggestion, the problem-setter would have to restrict the real world (no helicopters, no bridge, no material for a raft, etc.), in order to keep the puzzle on an even keel. The machine, however, lacks both the knowledge of the real world needed for this type of solution and the insight required to interpret that knowledge. Nor does it possess the necessary common sense to distinguish between possible, probable and far-fetched solutions.

Since we can currently eliminate such common sense and insight as an attribute of computer-driven intelligence, AI systems are reduced to expert systems (ES) or knowledge-based systems (KBS). Assumptions are made in advance about the nature of the world and the limitations of the framework within which the system will be used. AI in its current form is therefore not, as many people might suppose it to be, an objective form of knowledge manipulation, but a highly subjective and task-oriented one.

The General Structure of a KBS

The architecture of a typical knowledge processing ES can be broken down into the eight major components shown in Fig. 13 (Raulefs, 1985).

According to this model, the basic subsystems required for knowledge processing in expert systems may be summarized as follows:

1. The INFERENCE MACHINE which controls and executes all reasoning directed towards achieving the respective goals. Here, inferences are performed by the deduction system and/or by a simulation system which in turn is managed by the control system. Both deductions and simulations are sequences of inference steps or state transitions carried out according to specific rules or models. These rules or models are supplied by

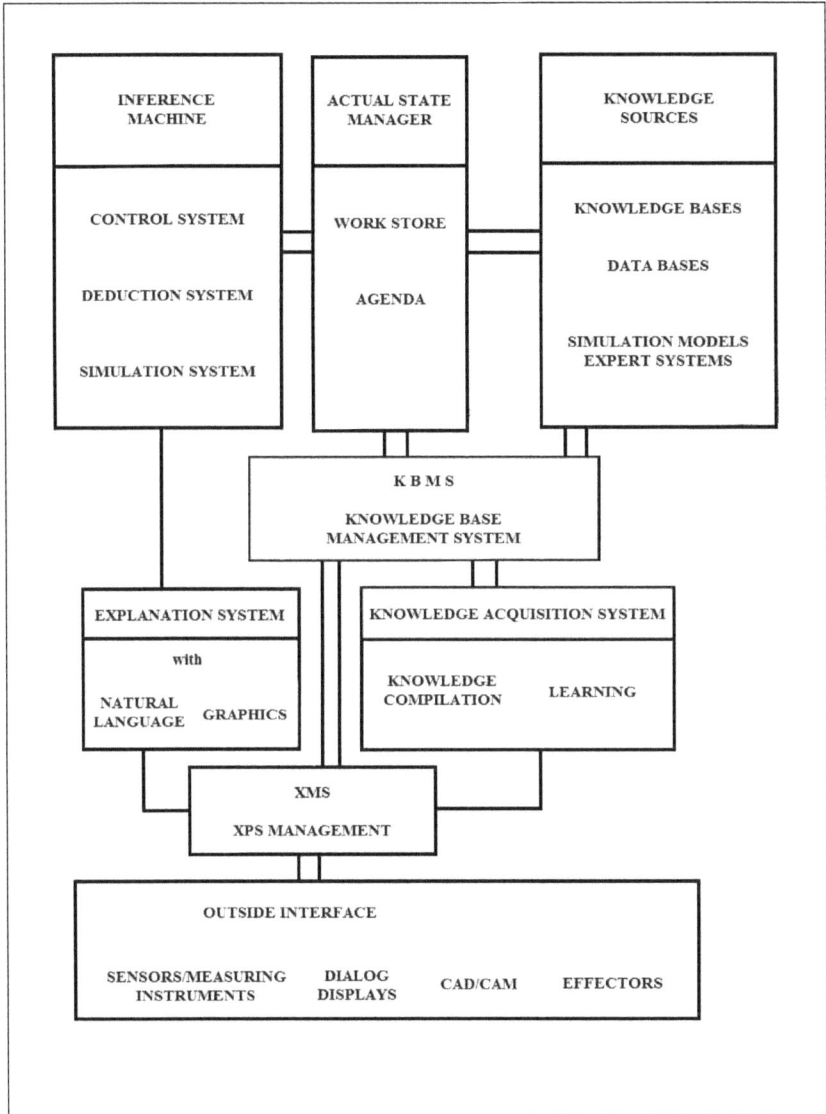

Fig. 13. Typical architecture of a knowledge-based expert system

2. KNOWLEDGE SOURCES which comprise a base of factual knowledge extracted from such sources as conventional database systems, simulations and other expert systems,

3. The ACTUAL STATE MANAGER, which is the subsystem responsible for maintaining intermediary results for use in subsequent processing stages and handling the information passed on for the purposes of updating a knowledge source or preparing data output.

4. The information flow in the Actual State Manager and the exploitation of its various components are handled by the KNOWLEDGE BASE MANAGEMENT SYSTEM (KBMS).

5. The user of the EXPERT SYSTEM is kept informed of the current processes by the EXPLANATION SYSTEM, which provides user information on several levels of abstraction.

6. Knowledge gathering and assimilation is handled by the KNOWLEDGE ACQUISTION SYSTEM, which is used for handling and compiling incoming knowledge from a variety of sources.

7. OUTSIDE INTERFACES enable communication between expert system cases and examples.

8. All of these subsystems are supervised and controlled by the XMS or EXPERT SYSTEM MANAGEMENT SYSTEM, which serves as a central switchboard for all other internal subsystems.

The Role of the Knowledge Engineer

It is clear that the tasks involved in the effective manipulation of real-world knowledge and their representation through a single human language necessitate solutions at the limits of current software technology. Such systems have currently reached the stage where specific, isolated problems can be successfully solved if the required domain of expertise is clearly defined and the knowledge incorporated into the expert system is quantifiable and undisputed. Furthermore, the knowledge required for the expert system to reach the level of competence required must be accessible and capable of being represented without accounting for causal functional and structural relationships with the system itself.

The interface between the expert system and its environment must be clearly confined to formalized man-machine interactions, such as the input of measured and easily interpretable sensory data. An efficient interface between the machine-language (ML) and the user's human or natural language (NL) is a requirement which is already straining the abilities of current expert systems. In my view, however, even this goal is a modest one, for successful CAEFL applications require a dual or multi-language ML/NL interface, a requirement which is clearly not served by one-to-one concordance or domain-tagging translation systems. Indeed, it is necessary to aim for a degree of deep reasoning in areas of language in which parsing and quantifying by traditional methods are inadequate.

The issues involved in implementing an expert system are discussed by Rees (1985) of Digital Equipment who cites the stages set out below as being required to effectively build and use an expert system for the practical application of artificial intelligence.

1. Select the right problem.

2. Identify an expert with the necessary expertise.

3. Create a knowledge engineer.

4. Create effective management for the development and introduction process.

5. Acquire the tool, i.e. hardware, software and services.

Conventional techniques work well with problems that can be expressed and solved arithmetically or algorithmically, but expert systems are called for when the application of intelligence and knowledge are required. At Digital Equipment, research has been primarily in the field of business applications and the knowledge engineers thus created are therefore those from a business background. The implication for CALL applications, however, would be that the knowledge engineer in the implementation of a CALL expert system should be an experienced teacher.

The knowledge engineer has the task of translating the working methods of the expert into a computerized system. This model works fine in the case of business or even technical applications where the expert and the knowledge engineer can view the system from both the point of view of software engineer and user. However, a teacher who may possess recognized expertise and may be entrusted with the task of developing a CALL expert system, can by definition not be regarded as an expert user. Here, the expert user is the student, who, however, does not possess expert knowledge and therefore could not become a knowledge engineer, even if they so wished. Clearly, it is not possible in a CALL development environment to equate the expert with the knowledge engineer, rather the knowledge engineer should work as closely as possible with as broad a base as possible of expert users (students) in order to engage in participative design. After consultation with the experts, the knowledge engineer encodes rules, verifies them with the expert and modifies them as required, providing a closed feedback loop of experimentation and implementation as shown in Fig. 14.

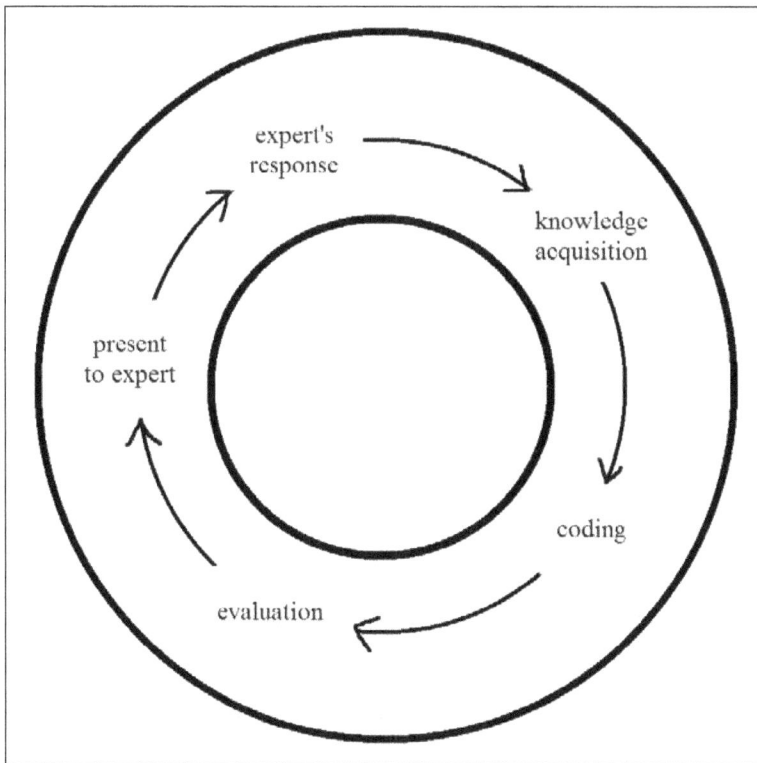

Fig. 14. The activities of a knowledge engineer (Rees, 1985)

In an ideal world in which one strives for perfection, it would be impossible to break out of this development loop, and indeed it can be argued that the ultimate task of the perfectionist software engineer is to delay implementation indefinitely, thus ensuring a perfect product implemented at infinity. In practice, prototypes must be issued and implemented at some stage short of perfection.

Deep Knowledge

Raulefs (1985) identifies the lack of deep reasoning as a major deficiency of current expert systems. In other words, existing expert systems employ only shallow knowledge by 'associating chunks of propositional with pieces of inferential knowledge without explicitly representing why and how this is related to the structure and function of the system being reasoned about.' Current expert systems do not 'know' what they are doing in the sense that they can reason about it or deal with unexpected situations. Deep knowledge is required to open up broader areas, where judgmental and experiential (shallow) knowledge serve to determine inferences which would require extensive searching if deep knowledge were to be used. Shallow knowledge can, however, be compiled from deep knowledge, and the second generation of expert systems now under development strive to incorporate both deep knowledge and shallow or compiled knowledge.

Cooperative Access Systems

Wahlster (1985) describes the development of cooperative access systems designed to act as interfaces between NL on the one hand and database systems, expert systems, operating systems, CAD systems and even text formatting systems on the other. In order to exhibit cooperative behaviour, a system requires relevant conceptual and inferential knowledge; it must have a model of the user with whom it is to cooperate and must be in a position to understand the goals and actions of this user and be able to adapt its behaviour accordingly. Cooperative behaviour in the sense the term is used by Wahlster is very close to the behaviour of a language teacher in the classroom, in that they respond not only to the superficial meaning (and grammatical correctness) of a student utterance, but draws implications from each utterance and contributes to the learning process by making deductions and inferences about the students' state of knowledge and linguistic ability. Similarly, in response to a question posed by a student, the teacher will often provide an explanation which goes far beyond the scope of the original question, contextualizing the question and supplementing the answer by providing knowledge not specifically requested. Wahlster's examples are not taken from language teaching situations, but parallels to the ELT classroom experience can clearly be drawn. In the following series of interchanges, U represents the User of a system, C the responses of a cooperative system and S the responses of a conventional system. The headings indicate the supplemental functions of a cooperative system.

Pointing out incorrect presuppositions:

U: *Did Mr. Jones pay the bill for our last delivery?*

C: *No, we have not yet sent Mr. Jones the bill.*

S: No. (Misleading conclusion)

Indication of discontinuities in the database:

U: Is there a seat available on the flight to New York on August 8th?

C: Yes, but from August 9th onwards, tickets are $200 cheaper due to the winter season.

S: Yes. (Unfriendly response)

Unsolicited justification of an answer:

U: Is a long-term fixed money investment worthwhile at the moment?

C: No, because interests are tending to rise.

S: No. (Missing argumentation)

Additional information on the individual conjuncts:

U: Are Mr. Brown and Mr. Gray on a business trip?

C: No, Mr. Brown is on a business trip but Mr. Gray is here.

S: No. (Answer provoking follow-up questions)

Unsolicited filling of the relevant deep case:

U: Which colleagues are on business trips?

C: Mr. Baker is in London, Mr. Miller is in New York and Mr. Smith is in Japan.

S: Mr. Baker, Mr. Miller and Mr. Smith. (Answer provoking follow-up questions)

Offering to 'monitor' for information requested;

U: Is there a seat available on the last flight from Munich to Hamburg?

C: *No, not at the moment, but I will put you on the waiting list and I will let you know if a passenger cancels his flight.*

S: *No.* (Unfriendly response)

Using more specific quantifiers:

U: *Are you employing some researchers with a Ph.D., too?*

C: *Yes, three.*

S: *Yes.* (Less cooperative response)

An experienced EFL teacher will immediately recognize the staccato responses of a conventional system. They are precisely the skeletal responses one receives so often in the classroom and strives to avoid. A machine used for teaching NL must clearly reach the cooperative level in order to provide a useful model for the student during dialog interaction. It is in this respect that the adventure games discussed in Part One reach their limitation. As has been seen, they not only fail to stimulate authentic interaction but can even be destructive by encouraging the use of minimal linguistic formulations. And yet, in their own way, these simple programs, too, are expert systems, possessing deep knowledge in a predetermined and limited subject area. Whether the scenario is a real one, such as flying an aircraft, or an imaginary one, such as embarking on a quest in an adventure game, does not affect the functional principles of the program.

The Structure of Natural Language Dialog Systems

The various strategies for making expert system natural language interfaces cooperative (recognition of presupposition violations, providing additional information on individual conjuncts, filling relevant deep cases, etc.), indicate clearly the functions lacking from existing CALL systems. Wahlster's model for formalizing natural language is illustrated in Fig. 15.

In this knowledge-based model, an analysis component translates the natural language input into a formal semantic representation, drawing on a knowledge base of general, domain-specific and dialog-based knowledge elements. Dialog- based knowledge includes a user model containing information about the user and an inference memory enabling the system to explain the reasoning underlying its answers. The evaluation component receives the semantic representation of an input and accesses both the knowledge base and any external data sources relevant to the task in hand (e.g. a database). A generation component translates the formal semantic representation of the output from the evaluation component into a natural language utterance comprehensible to the user.

It would be possible to adapt this model to make it applicable to a language learning environment simply by treating the subject matter (the target language) as domain-specific knowledge. This, however, overlooks the fact that language acquisition is concerned at least as much with skills as with knowledge, and since a teacher of a foreign language in a single-language environment is also able to draw on parallels between L1 (human source language) and L2 (human target language) and is often able to translate freely between them as required, the model would become more complicated, as can be seen from schematic diagram in Fig. 16.

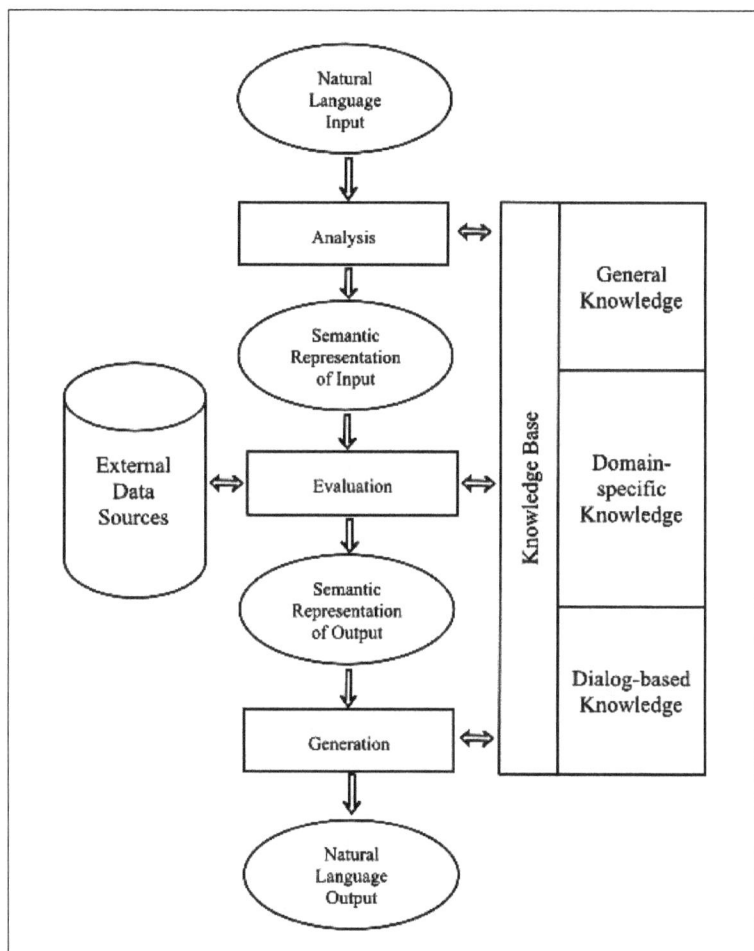

Fig. 15. The overall structure of NL dialog systems

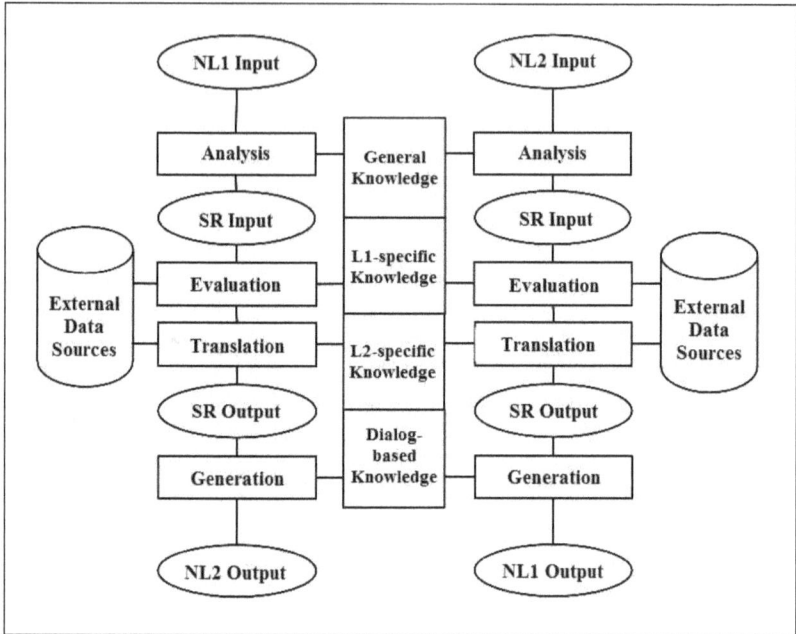

Fig. 16. The overall structure of a dual natural language dialog system

Whereas the system described by Wahlster has been realized (Hoeppner et al., 1984) in the system HAM-ANS, the dual-human language model does not, as yet, exist.

If, however, we regard L2 as an expert system in itself, then the task at hand is that of providing an NL interface to L2. Fig. 17 shows the architecture of an NL interface to expert systems in which there are two separate knowledge bases, one for the natural language interface and a second for the expert system. By taking advantage of this separation, one might adapt the system for the task of accessing L2 by treating L2 content as task-specific knowledge. However, a mirror-image interface is now required in order to cope with the NL complexities of L2.

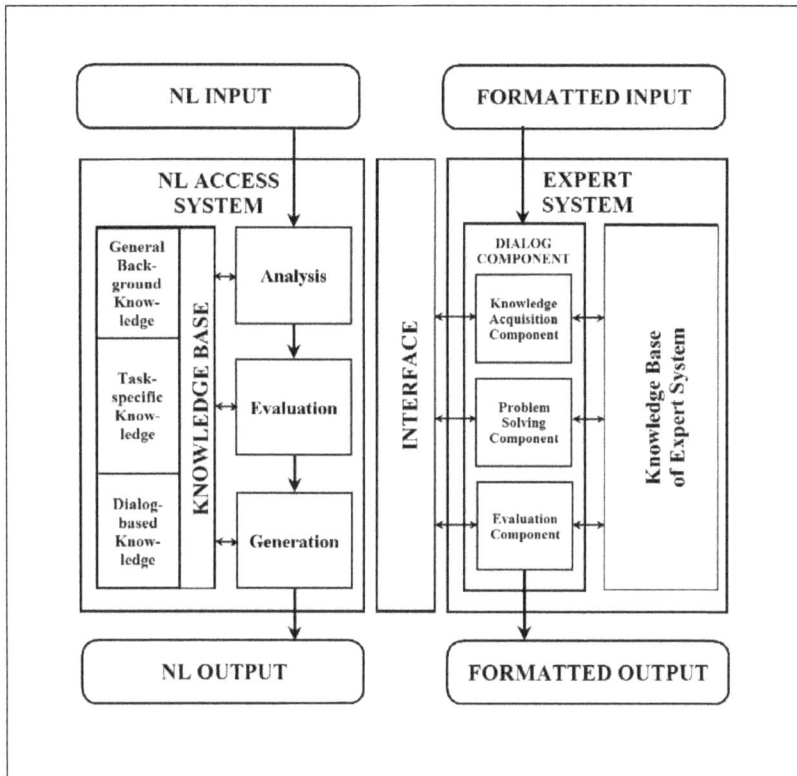

Fig. 17. The architecture of a natural language interface to expert systems

Currently, even single-Language NL interfaces are not yet in a position to offer broad-based universal language capabilities comparable to human dialog partners, but at least a start has been made in this direction, and a model such the one as shown above could represent the logical next step in the development of interactive CALL systems.

Why, then, in the light of the developments in hardware and comparative excellence of software in other areas, are the currently available language teaching programs so limited? The answer to this must be sought in the very nature of human language itself; computers in their current state can handle tasks which can effectively be split into sub-tasks which in turn can be carried out by reference to a fixed set of rules. Everything in this model is explicit and unambiguous. Human interaction, however, is often implicit and ambiguous; a given word has no fixed meaning outside a specific context. This is a problem for the lexicographer, the translator and the language teacher alike. Attempts at implementing a computer to fulfil the requirements normally carried out by a human language teacher therefore face different problems to those faced by expert systems in other areas.

The requirement of AI applications for large amounts of virtual memory and the necessity to dynamically manipulate vast amounts of data from a variety of sources have placed very heavy demands on the environment used to support development of AI applications. Various programming styles have developed out of this situation, such as rule-based programming, metaprogramming (embedding new languages and control structures in the host language), data-driven programming, logic-based programming and object-oriented programming. New software tools are rapidly being developed and proven programming languages such as Smalltalk, Objtalk, Lisp, CLOS are now in widespread use for the development of such software applications as hypertext and hypermedia which in terms of flexibility of application and dependence on interconnectivity share a broadness of conceptuality akin to the characteristics of a natural language interface.

An insight into the problems to be faced by future software engineers confronted with the task of developing efficient

CAEFL programs may be obtained by a study of the current state of NL text manipulation systems.

The Siemens TINA text content analysis project aimed to develop linguistically based processes and methods to support automatic preprocessing of natural language data with respect to real world information processing. A set of procedures and modules were developed to cope with various applications such as text analysis, information retrieval and NL interfaces to databases. One tool developed to this end was the morphological retrieval tool MARS (Morphological Analysis for Retrieval Support, Niedermair, 1984). MARS utilizes morphological decomposition during search (as opposed to grapheme or string-based decomposition and search routines. Thus it is the task of this tool to break a word down into its morphological components and use these as a basis for search operations. Thus the term 'electrically-heated' would be decomposed into the elements (electric)/ally/-/(heat)/ed, enabling the system to search for related words based on the roots (identified here by brackets) such as electricity or heating, in other words, a function approaching the kind of linguistic manipulation and association which an experienced language teacher would carry out almost instinctively. A further Siemens Tool, COPSY (Context Operator Syntax, C. Schwarz, 1984) performs a similar retrieval task on the basis of syntactic decomposition, extracting the syntax of a search query and matching its normalized form with the syntactical structures contained in the database being searched. Any teacher who has taught grammar will be familiar with this process in NL, but its implementation in machine text processing is so far very limited.

Since second-language teaching is closely linked to the concept of code-switching (translation either from or into the students' native language), it is useful in this context to consider the state of the art in computer assisted translation or 'Machine Translation' as it is still often referred to. Software currently available for the home computer or PC market are at the best primitive word-for-word translation programs (electronic dictionaries) and at the worst completely misleading. Even professional software/hardware combinations currently on offer leave much to be desired.

The human language teacher may choose from a number of resources for the teaching of a foreign language, and may elect to teach variously by grammatical explanation (syntax-focused), by direct method teaching (experience-based), by practice and drilling (repetition-based), functional/notional (activity-based) or by translation (specific practical application based). A bilingual teacher may move between these methods frequently during a single lesson, but each of these functions represents a considerable hurdle for his mechanical counterpart. The art of translation is a key skill here, too, although no longer in such widespread use as a method of teaching as in previous years, but nevertheless a very important part of language learning and very often a useful shortcut in the teaching/learning process. Regrettably, machine translation is still in its infancy, and although a large number of translation companies now boast a computer assisted translation service, the procedure is slow and inefficient and the results far from impressive. At best, such systems are capable of producing a rough draft to be edited by an experienced translator. The problem here is largely one of syntax and context recognition. As electronic dictionaries, such systems as METAL are a very useful aid to the inexperienced translator, but even when I tested the latest version available at the time of writing, the system was slow, unimpressive and required very careful handling. Context identification is largely achieved by tagging various translations of individual words, so that the user must identify the subject area before implementing the system, which then translates all words within the context of that subject area. The average time taken to 'learn' a new word is between five and ten minutes and even after careful tagging, it is all too easy to catch the machine out. The majority of work still falls to the human editor, who very probably experiences the same emotions as a teacher marking unimpressive examination scripts, a non-sought-after reversal of roles. It is probably best to see the current state of the art of machine translations as efficient symbiotic systems in embryo rather than as a form of AI at all. When regarded as fully automatic systems, all machine translation programs fail so badly that their practical value is questionable. The latest claim by the manufacturers is 80 % correctness at sentence level, in other words, the most optimistic claim is that the machine produces 20 % pure garbage.

The main problem here is the nature of human language when contrasted to the standard procedural limitations of the computer. Neither a purely algorithmic approach, such as that employed by the designers of vocabulary tutors, nor a semi-heuristic communication interface as found in the games programs discussed, represents an adequate approach. Tools and methodologies are required which enable the programmer to produce an integrated dual-language communication environment. In this context, it is of interest to look to the most recent developments in software design techniques, in particular to the benefits offered by object-oriented software design and development environments.

Object-Oriented Software Design and Development

We have so far referred to the concept of object-oriented design and development (OOSD) only in rather general terms, so let me now set out the main principles involved in more specific terms. Put briefly, the goals of OOSD may be summarized as follows:

1.   Fulfilment of user expectations

2.   Consistency

3.   Simplicity

4.   Integration

5.   Visual perception support

6.   Direct manipulation

7.   Modelessness

8. Customizability

9.   Reusability

10. Polymorphism

Object-oriented design and development promotes reusability techniques by data abstraction, inheritance and division of superclasses into subclasses. The polymorphism of objects increases both customizability and reusability.

Optimum functionality is attained when OOSD is employed in accordance with the Law of Good Style (The Law of Demeter), which states:

> *For all classes C, and for all methods M attached to C, all objects to which M sends a message must be instances of classes associated with the following classes:*
>
> *1. Objects created by M*
> *2. Instance variable classes of C.*

This interdependency of classes and objects may be viewed as a parallel to the polymorphic class hierarchy of human language. The failure of vocabulary tutor programs (and indeed of traditional dictionaries) to do full justice to the variety of overlapping L1/L2 equivalence classes is evident in the dictionary structure consisting largely of direct equivalents, a problem only partly solved in such systems as METAL by tagging subject areas.

Thus the English word 'joint' may have a simple dictionary entry such as 'Verbindung', or a multiple entry tagged by subject area, but either of these treatments fails to register the dependency of classes in either L1 or L2, let alone the interdependencies between them. Such a dependency is illustrated in Fig. 18, although the diagram itself has been somewhat simplified.

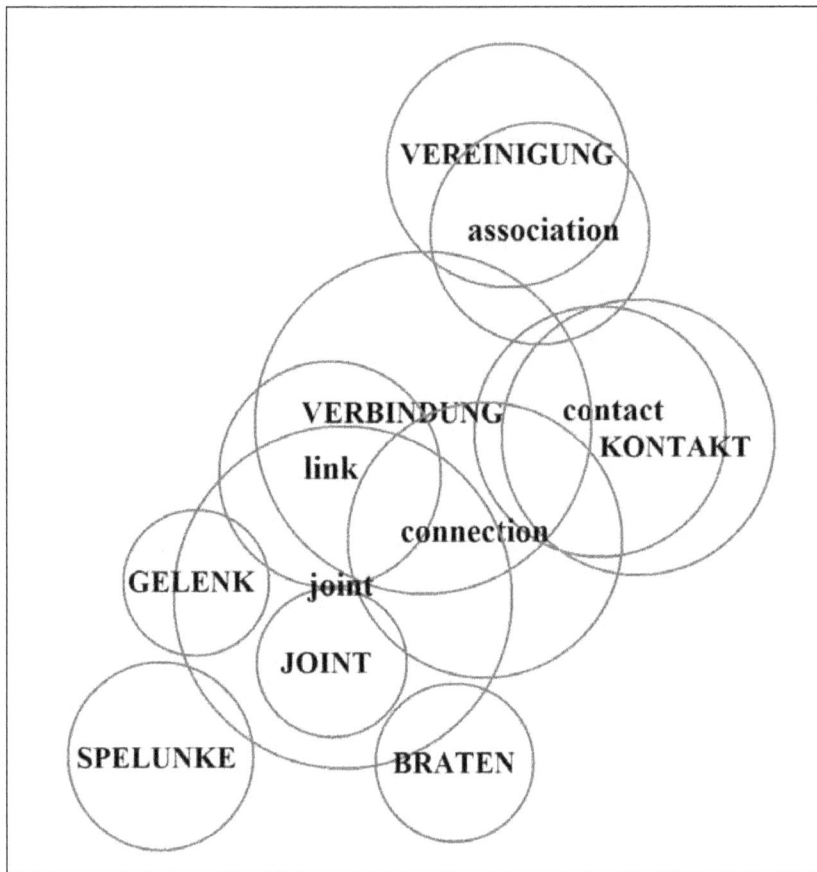

Fig. 18. Lexical concordance sets around 'joint' and 'VERBINDUNG'
(lower case = English; upper case = German)

In practice, I often draw on such parallels to set theory in my own class teaching – usually to good effect – but no such concepts have yet been incorporated into any commercially available CAEFL programs.

Expert Systems and CALL

Radig's (1986) distinction between the expert's and the user's approach to the application of expert systems indirectly sheds light on the problems involved in the development of CALL programs. From an expert's point of view, an ES is a tool which helps to analyse and codify domain knowledge, makes such knowledge available to others and facilitates the pooling of knowledge from different domains. From the user's point of view, an expert system can assume various roles. It can be a 'limited human expert imitator', a colleague, an assistant or a substitute human. In the field of CALL applications, the ES is a human imitator inasmuch as it has the function of simulating a teacher or at least fulfilling some of the same functions (instruction, task definition, assessment, correction), but to be effective, it must also adopt the role of a colleague or peer, pursuing a path of discovery, checking the user's reasoning and reminding them of alternative solutions.

This role also merges into that of assistant, freeing the user from 'boring elaboration of hypothetical solutions and providing support in areas which are not central to the problem' (ibid.). A built-in grammar or spelling checker could, for example, liberate a user from certain mundane linguistic activities which are not part of the specific task in hand during the text input phase of a teaching program; language exercises can be produced automatically using vocabulary from the vocabulary base in conjunction with user-defined constraints and patterns. The user of an ES in this context is, of course, the teacher-programmer, not the student, who is the user of the program developed with the aid of the expert system.

The key advantages of an ES may be summed up as follows:

1. They provide a solid base of knowledge in their subject areas and do not overlook relevant information.

2. They offer high-performance, handling a vast amount of information simultaneously.

3. They are selective and can pick out relevant data from the general information flow.

4. Within limits, they learn from experience and do not make the same mistake twice – provided the cause of the mistake can be traced to specific knowledge chunks.

5. They offer consistency and the ability to resolve conflicting constraints in a consistently reproducible way.

6. They have stamina. They can follow long and complicated reasoning chains where humans tend to get lost.

When applied to tasks in engineering or marketing, these are highly significant advantages. When taking into account the linguistic manipulation required by effective language teaching, however, these advantages need to be taken in context. The main obstacle is the traditional dependence of ES on knowledge bases. The knowledge base alone is inadequate for language teaching, even in humans; otherwise every speaker of a second language would make an excellent teacher. An intelligent system requires an intelligent user interface, providing intelligent behaviour towards the user, whereby it not only arrives at a solution to the user's problem but also provides suitable explanations and arguments. The ability to interact with the user in the latter's natural language is regarded as an essential step in increasing the acceptance of expert systems.

Expert System Shells

The development of expert system shells (XPS) is an important trend in this respect, since an XPS provides the means of avoiding a domain-oriented or machine-specific metalanguage when using the computer as a problem solver. In practical use, XPS may be implemented for a variety of purposes and once a database has been established, the XPS is used to handle the NL/ML interchange. The Nixdorf shell (Savory, 1985) offers reusability within a limited area (initially that of technical fault finding), with the additional facility of an English to German translation of the DB output via the XPS. It is the function of the human expert to construct a KB tree, such as that shown in Fig. 19, of the interrelated cases which will form the basis of any given consultation.

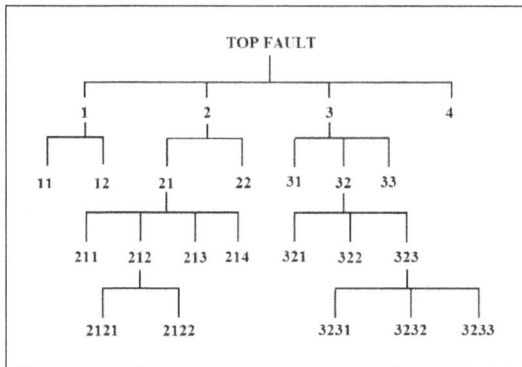

Fig. 19. Typical FF tree for the KB of the Nixdorf XPS shell

In the fault finding (FF) application, the dialog is initiated by the ES whilst the user's response is largely limited to 'yes' and 'no'. This alone would not constitute an expert system, but together with the other functions offered, this shell approaches the SW goals of the ES engineer. At any branching point, the user is offered the opportunity to

1. Ask 'why' if they do not understand.

2. Demand a status report.

3. Request help if they get lost.

4. Tell the system to change its focus or context ('hint' function).

5. Communicate in different languages (English, German, etc.).

6. Provide synonyms as answers.

7. Ask what answers are possible.

8. Preview the causes of any fault.

In addition, the system offers

9. Automatically generated narrative knowledge base documentation

10. Elementary graphics output for simple sketches

11. Analytical summaries of all FF runs.

In particular, points one through seven are clearly adaptable for use by CAEFL software engineer and the XPS could form a useful communications interface in this context. Of special interest for tutoring purposes are the 'why' and 'hint' functions. In 'hint', the user can take over control of the dialog flow to check out a theory concerning possible solutions to the task in hand. In the Nixdorff FF application of the shell, this enables the user to break into the flow at any branching point and guess at the top fault. In a CAEFL application, this could be a particularly valuable time-saver.

The knowledge base (KB) for the Nixdorf XPS is constructed as a series of PROLOG clauses holding constructional, relational and generic data. The examples below are taken from the field of electromechanical devices.

```
cable (rpc-cable, smc-drive, smc-rpc-panel,
smcrpc-slot).
clamped (rpc-cable).
holds (safety-detents, smc-drive).
is-a-sort-of (smc-drive, telescope-mounted).
is-safe (screwed-cable).
makes-safe (mains-switch, rear, mains-cable).
obstructs (smc-drive, rear, rear-door).
opening-tool (door, a-key, unlock).
posn (rpc-cable, upper-left, left,
peripheralschassis).
```

The knowledge declared in this way is of various types and may be generic, i.e. independent of a particular device, or hardware specific. Specific knowledge must, however, be assigned to a generic class. The generic knowledge contained in the declaration of an 'opening-tool'

```
opening-tool (door, a-key, unlock).
```

consists of the predicate name, stating the implied action (e.g. opening), the generic object type (e.g. the class of doors) and the tool used to perform the action on that particular object class (a-key). Finally, the imperative form of the appropriate verb (unlock) is added as a further parameter to specify more precisely the particular action associated with using the tool on the object.

In the following declaration

```
is-a-sort-of (main-switch, switch).
```

a specific object (main-switch) is assigned to a generic class of object types (switch).

Domain-specific (here, device-specific) knowledge may be used to store knowledge about the relative positions of objects. Thus the declaration

```
posn(rpc-cable, upper-left, left,
peripheralschassis).
```

defines the relative position of the repeater cable within its immediate environment, stating that it is located in the upper left corner of the left side of the peripherals chassis.

Relative attributes may be expressed in other ways, e.g.

```
cable(rpc-cable, smc-drive, smc-rpc-panel,
smc-rpc-slot).
```

also defining the units to which the cable is attached. Further predicates are used to store data about methods of attachment:

```
clamped (rpc-cable).
```

difficulty of access:

```
obstructs (smc-drive, rear, rear-door).
```

and safety factors:

```
is-safe (screwed-cable).
makes-safe (mains-switch, rear, mains-
cable).
```

Knowledge bases stored in this way can be processed by the XPS to generate narrative documentation tracing all paths through the knowledge, optionally in English or German.

In the Nixdorf FF application, the computer is being used as an electronic technician's manual, guiding the repairman through a fault-finding process. If the human expert has had access to all the relevant information at the stage of establishing the KB then there should be very little need to deviate from the standard branching provided for by the KB tree. The actual fault finding process itself is strictly algorithmic and requires very little computing power. Of great interest to the CAEFL designer, however, is the shell's ability to handle NL input and output in more than one language. The ability of the XPS to accept synonyms and abbreviated forms approaches NL interaction. Furthermore, the 'why' and 'hint' functions could be expanded to transform the role of the user from a passive answer-seeker to an active dialog partner. The real problem, however, lies in defining the environment of the real world for NL communication purposes. In the closed environment of, for example, electromechanical devices, it is possible to declare the attributes of a cable or a tool in relation to their location or function, but it is a completely different matter to catalogue all the uses to which, say, a knife, could be put (to cut, to threaten, to remove stones from a shoe, etc.) and to order the KB in a coherent and accessible way.

Natural Language versus Machine Language

Although the purposes of autonomous language learning can to an extent be served by the mentoring provided by the direct input/output type of program considered in Part One, the closer a machine language interface can simulate a human teacher, the more authentic and satisfying the learning experience becomes. This requires software which can process both knowledge about the user and knowledge of the real world whilst handling a communication process which is not in itself obtrusive. It should not be necessary for a new user of a system to have to relearn everything that they have previously known about communication simply because an automated system is now being used to assume a role which was previously the prerogative of a human being. However, this is precisely the situation with which we are frequently confronted. It is often necessary for even the specialist, after a given period of time, to 'relearn' and adapt to a new communications process. Ideally, the human user should be the 'fixpoint' for the design of human-computer systems (Fischer, 1986). User-centred system design (Norman & Draper,

1986) starts on the outside by taking into consideration the overall environment, social, technical and otherwise, and then progressing through psychological and behavioural aspects of human life inwards towards specific technical considerations (Fig. 20).

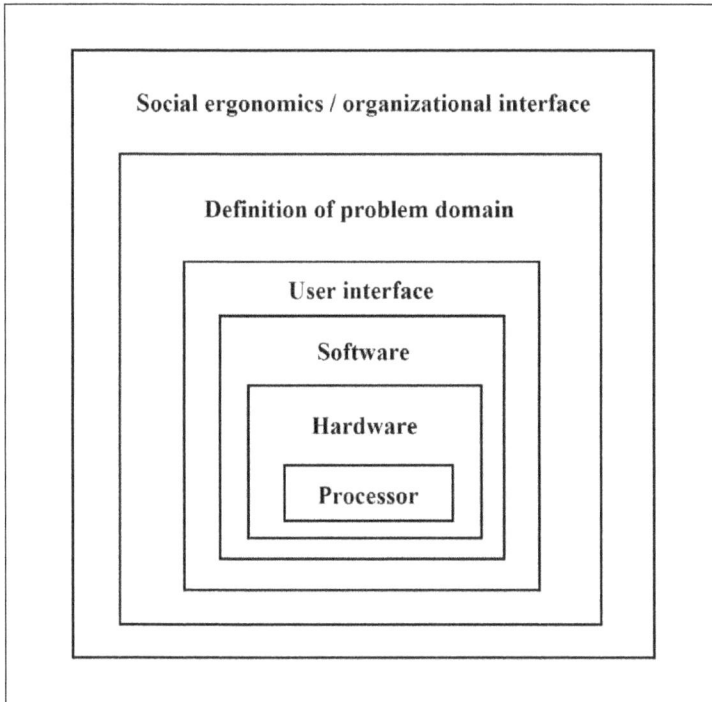

Fig. 20. System development from the outside to the inside
(cf. Fischer, 1986)

Cognitive Language Learning

In CAEFL as in other areas of SW implementation, the majority of systems are computer-centred rather than user-centred and therefore fail to meet the actual needs of the target group. In this context we have already observed the distinction between cognitive language learning and revelatory or experiential language acquisition and dwelt to some extent on the latter aspect. I would now like to turn in rather more detail to the cognitive domain. Cognitive science is a discipline which combines a group of related disciplines such as psychology, linguistics, sociology and philosophy, and has been defined (Simon, 1980) as 'the domain of inquiry that seeks to understand intelligent systems and the nature of intelligence'. I have already briefly discussed the nature of intelligence and as we have seen, it is questionable whether the Turing test is still valid today. Let us, therefore, consider the nature of 'intelligent systems' and how information processing by machines differs from information processing by humans.

In normal language communication, humans can

1. Convey information

2. Benefit from each other's knowledge and abilities

3. Influence each other's behaviour

4. Deduce implicit information other than knowledge consciously conveyed

5. Process conflicting information

6. Continually revise information previously conveyed

7. Reject false or misleading information

8. Resolve paradoxes

Attempts have been made to establish qualitative design criteria for the development of human-computer communication systems which take into account the differences in information processing between humans and computers (Fischer, 1986). By establishing and implementing such criteria, we come a step closer to the goal of producing a workable NL/ML interface suitable for autonomous language learning. Let us therefore try to establish some reasonable axioms applicable to the design of such interfaces.

Whereas it is generally accepted that computers are efficient at handling vast amounts of information, it is not actually the quantity of information available that creates constraints in human information processing, but rather the limitations of human attention and comprehension. Not only the access to information, but its meaningful selection is therefore an important aspect of human/computer systems. On a Boeing 747 there 455 separate warnings signals (Chambers & Nagel, 1985). In such a case, information overload can only be avoided by implementing technologies which select and establish priorities before issuing warnings to the crew.

In many cases, real-world problems are so complex and changeable that the search for an optimum rational solution may in some cases be quite futile. Rather than seek ultimate solutions, the goal of human/computer systems should be to extend the boundaries of human rationality and overcome the constraints of human knowledge, recollection and reasoning. A pragmatic approach is required in which ideal solutions are not always sought, but in which solutions are striven for which are workable and adaptable to dynamically changing circumstances.

The limitations inherent in human memory patterns and human thought processes must be taken into account in designing human/computer communication systems. When developing ostensibly authentic and realistic dialog interfaces, it is not meaningful to replicate the limitations we are striving to overcome. In this sense, the computer may to a certain extent be seen as an artificial extension of our intellect serving to extend human thought processes and memory by processing and storing information beyond the scope of a single human being.

As has already been observed in my discussion of PC CAEFL programs, traditional screen output displays consist of a two-dimensional textual representation and thus fail to exploit the efficient visual processing capabilities of the human. The technology now exists, however, to add an extra visual element to human/computer interaction by means of multi-window technologies, colour displays, graphics, icons, animation and sound. Human/computer interfaces should therefore exploit this key potential.

It is essential for the structure of the computer system to be comprehensible to users rather than requiring them to learn a limited range of fixed functions by rote. Learning by rote makes it difficult for the user to deal with unexpected occurrences and inhibits originality. Furthermore, it is a misconception that there is a single 'user' of any given system. This is no more true in human/computer interaction than it is in the classroom. There is no single 'student' for whom a perfect textbook can be written. Rather, there are many different kinds of students to whom a human teacher must adapt his material and techniques. And this technique, too, must be modified as the student's needs change. Similarly, in the case of a human/computer interface, the requirements of each individual user may differ and may change and expand with experience. The demands of a dynamic user community cannot therefore be met by computer systems based on a static model of an archetypal user.

We have already referred to a shift in perspective which has led to the view of the computer as a device for symbolic manipulation rather than for computation. This in turn makes it necessary to develop concepts about information processing which can be used to analyse information processing techniques in humans as well as in machines. Programming languages provide formalisms which enable us to enhance our under-standing of human cognitive functions. Thus a successfully designed and implemented XPS in itself represents a deepening of our comprehension and brings us closer to the goal of understanding the communication (and therefore the learning) process in humans and consequently closer to producing really meaningful CALL programs.

Symbiotic systems have already been mentioned in the context of machine translation. Such systems are based on the notion that some tasks can be best carried out by utilizing a com-bination of computer and human skills. Thus the combined computing power of the machine and the insight of its human counterpart can solve problems and carry out tasks which neither the one nor the other could achieve alone. Despite claims to the contrary and the occasional breakthrough in computerized problem-solving, all present expert systems and embryonic artificial intelligence programs are in reality symbiotic systems, not autonomous ones. In the light of this, the human/ computer interface takes on an even greater significance. Every computer user is familiar with the occasional breakdown in communication caused by either a technical defect in the machine (resulting from an inadequate magnetic track, perhaps, or an unacceptable reduction in system voltage), or by a lapse of memory or gap in the knowledge on the part of the user (e.g. forgetting or not knowing the syntax for a command or expression), but an actual difference of 'opinion' between the computer and the human remains the stuff of science fiction, except inasmuch as knowledge-based systems incorporate the will and understanding of their designers.

Processing Fuzzy Concepts

In terms of human-computer interaction and autonomous computer assisted language learning, it is clear that the mere analysis and generation of on-screen textual representation is inadequate, so the focus of research shifts to problems of partner modelling, non-grammatical phrases and indirect speech acts (cf. also Wahlster, 1986). It is in this connection that I would now like to turn my attention to the notion of 'fuzzy concepts'. For the basis of the system of establishing a generalized assignment statement for dealing with fuzzy quantifiers and predicates, I am indebted to L. A. Zadeh of the Computer Science Division of the University of California at Berkeley (see bibliography), and I have endeavoured to extend this work further in order to construct a basis for designing an L1/L2 concordance assignment statement for incorporation into L1/ML/L2- based CAEFL language interfaces.

One of the greatest linguistic difficulties inherent in establishing a system of quantification for dealing with the real world is that many of our notions are in themselves not clearly defined. They are 'fuzzy concepts' and may be accorded not only a variety of meanings but a range of degree of meanings. The classical approaches to meaning representation are truth-conditional semantics, possible-world semantics and model-theoretic semantics (Tarski, 1956; Bartsch & Vennemann, 1972; Cresswell, 1973; Kamp, 1981). More recently, however, (Zadeh, 1982) the concept of test-score semantics has been developed in which a proposition, **p,** is seen as a collection of elastic constraints and its meaning represented as a procedure which tests, scores and aggregates the constraints associated with **p** resulting in a test score representing a measure of compatibility between **p** and the explanatory database (ED). The advantages of test-score semantics over such classical forms as those mentioned above can be found in the greater expressive power of this system of representation and its ability to handle fuzzy predicates and quantifiers such as 'old', 'near', 'most' and 'several' as well as fuzzy truth values (e.g. 'quite true', 'mostly true', 'generally false'). The search for a system of generalized assignment state-ments has led to a quantifiable system of constrained variables enabling the representation of an NL proposition as a collection of elastic constraints. Thus the general assignment statement in this scheme may be simplified as

X isr Q

in which **X** is the constrained variable, **Q** is the constraining object and **isr** is a copula in which **r** is a variable defining the role of **Q** in relation to **X**. Possible values of **r** are: **d** = disjunctive, **c** = conjunctive, **p** = probabilistic, **g** = granular and **h** = hybrid. In the examples below I have not, for the sake of clarity, adopted the convention by which the most common copula, the disjunctive **isd**, is reduced to **is**.

Clearly, it is also necessary to do justice to possible truth dependencies in NL, so conditional assignment statements must also be incorporated into this representation system, e.g.

$$X \text{ isr}_1 \ \Omega_1 \text{ if } Z \text{ isr}_2 \ \Omega_2$$

in which **Z** is a conditioning variable, Ω_2 is an object constraining **Z**, and **r1** and **r2** are variables defining the roles of Ω_1 and Ω_2 in relation to **X** and **Z** respectively.

Let us take the proposition

> **p: Mary left home sometime between four and five in the afternoon.** (Zadeh, 1986)

This may be represented as the generalized statement

$$X \text{ isd } [4pm \ 5pm]$$

whereas the conjunctive constraint in the proposition

> **p: Mary was at home from four to five in the afternoon. (ibid.)**

would be represented as

$$X \text{ isc } [4pm \text{ to } 5pm]$$

In order to quantify the elements of a given proposition in this way, it is necessary to establish an explanatory database in which each relation is an elastic constraint on the values of its attributes. The variable **X** which is constrained by **p** must then be identified and calculated for a given ED. Similarly, the constraint itself can be calculated as a function of the ED.

A proposition such as

Peter isd TALL

is clearly true if

X Height(Peter).

The fuzzy relation **TALL** is characterized by the membership function **µTALL**. The extent to which Peter is tall is then given by the degree **µTALL(h),** whereby **h** represents the numerical value of height. In other words **µTALL(h)** is the degree to which **h** fits the fuzzy predicate **TALL** in a given context. Having thus arrived at a method of quantifying fuzzy values, it is possible to use parsing techniques based on the numerical values involved to compare fuzzy values in two languages, providing a potential tool for constructing an effective ML/NL or L1/L2 interface and both machine translation and effective CAEFL programs come closer to being a reality.

In both the teaching of translation and teaching by translation (dual language method, L1/L2; L2/L1), it is often necessary to understand the hidden meaning of the source text. This in turn points to the necessity for a test-score analysis of the fuzzy quantifiers and predicates of the source language and matching them with possible target language variables in order to find the appropriate translation in the case of conjunctive constraints and the largest area of intersection in the case of disjunctive ones. Thus, whether the word 'recently' is to be translated into German as 'in der letzten Zeit', 'neulich', 'kürzlich', 'vor kurzem', or by some other word or phrase, will be determined by applying identical or similar test-score analysis procedures to LI and L2.

Let us now return to the proposition discussed above:

L1p1: X isd TALL

Assuming that the value of h has already been quantified in L1, converting the lexical items into their German equivalents would give rise to a number of possibie L2 propositions (assuming **X** to be a constant):

L2p1: X isd HOCH

L2p2: X isd GROSS

L2p3: X isd UNWAHR

each of which could be true depending on the nature of the constant **X** and the degree to which it fits a certain quantifiable criterion. Thus **L2p1** is true to extent to which **X** is an object such as a building, **L2p2** is true to the extent to which **X** is a person and **L2p3** to the extent to which it is a story.

The sole criterion here is therefore no longer the height **(h)** but the membership of **X** to the categories of person, objects and stories:

X isd GROSS if X PERSON

X isd HOCH if X BUILDING

X isd UNWAHR if X STORY

The extent to which **X** is a person is given by **μGROSS(p)** and the extent to which it is **HOCH** by **μHOCH(b)** and the extent to which it is a story by **μUNWAHR(s)**. If **p, b** and **s** are mutual exclusives, then the proposition can be seen as a granular constraint in L2:

X isg (GROSS, HOCH, UNWAHR)

and an NL translation assignment statement can be constructed accordingly:

if X isd TALL X isg [GROSS, HOCH, UNWAHR].

It must be borne in mind that no language teaching applications currently exist which adopt this procedure and that this representation system itself is still in a fairly early stage of development. A logical next step would be the incorporation of this system of dual language test-score semantic analysis into a generalized SW assignment statement to establish a manipulable series of class hierarchies, preferably using one of the OOSD languages previously discussed. This could then form the basis for a truly interactive dual NL/ML interface which in turn could represent the cornerstone of effective and intelligent CAEFL programs.

PART THREE

Conclusion and Appendixes

Conclusion from the First Edition

Despite the major advances in hardware generally and in software development techniques in certain areas, including NL and AI, it would appear that CALL and specifically CAEFL applications for autonomous learners have not kept pace with the general trend. Given the technical developments of recent years, we ought to have reached a high standard of development in language learning programs. Much potential, however, remains unrealized. Rather than embrace the complexity of human factors and strive for genuine user benefits, many technical innovations have been system-driven, with software being developed to underscore what the hardware can do rather than focus on what the user needs. Now that efficient graphic capabilities have been developed, they could be exploited to enhance language learning programs and take us beyond the limitations of enhanced text-based applications.

So what are the implications of this for language learning? Great technical advances have been made, more memory is available, but in many cases the language learning software currently available and currently being produced for autonomous learner use is little better in concept than the *ZX-80* demonstration program presented in Part One. Parsing has been improved somewhat, but the basic question and answer approach (in which the computer is always right) remains, whilst the possible forms of the answer are predetermined by the programmer in order to prevent the machine from seeming to make a fool of itself.

It can be seen, therefore, that substantially improved user interfaces are required before untrained users can communicate with a computer system via natural language and visual communication interfaces. However, once the software tools described in Part One of this book are combined with the theoretical concepts set out in Part Two, there is all reason to believe that the inadequacies of present language learning systems could be overcome in the near future.

Update 2020

For the sake of integrity, I have allowed the original conclusion, as set out above, to stand or fall on its merits and added the following remarks to bring the reader up to date with the current state of developments.

At the time the deliberations in this book were first set out, the topics of artificial intelligence and computer-aided learning were generally seen as future-oriented concepts; few people in the world of everyday ELT practice paid much attention to such matters, and the use of technology in the classroom was virtually non-existent. Similarly, little or no use was made of learning technologies by independent learners. To say that technology-enhanced learner autonomy and the use of artificial intelligence in language teaching were in their infancy is to overstate their importance at the time.

In the intervening years, we have certainly seen giant leaps in the technology available and most recently, the notion of artificial intelligence has become a frequent headline-grabber. Whether teaching methodologies have kept pace with technological advances is, however, another matter. The dominant form of instruction remains face-to-face teaching, even though technology may be used to bridge geographical hurdles, and in the majority of situations, the communicative approach continues to reign supreme. Technology is frequently used as a method of delivery, whether in the form of electronic whiteboards or instant messaging, or it provides a flexible platform for conventional teaching methods. The actual teaching is carried out by human teachers, whilst 'independent' learning frequently takes place under human supervision. Virtual worlds such as Second Life provide a wonderful opportunity for situational practice and even total immersion, but here, too, the central core is the human teacher. Why then have 'artificial intelligence' and 'virtual reality' recently become such fascinating buzz phrases.

Part of the answer is, I believe, to be sought in the downgrading of what these terms are taken to mean. At the time of my original research, artificial intelligence was not usually associated with language teaching or language learning but still bore echoes of the Turing Test. It had, however, already morphed into a less impressive knowledge-based system of systematic branching decisions and was being developed for the purposes of technical troubleshooting and providing automated assistance to helpline staff. Eventually, improvements in speech synthesizers and voice recognition systems would add a new dimension to what was in fact a set of well-established principles in technological terms. And it is precisely this add-on, the functionality of being able to speak to a machine and get an intelligible (if not intelligent) answer, that has seized the public imagination and set science fiction writers off in a new burst of robotics-based fantasy. In a sense, artificial intelligence has not made the great leap that many observers suppose; on the contrary, the concept has simply been downgraded to describe what we could already do before, but since we can now do it faster and more impressively, it creates the impression of a more intelligent system. What we have is not more intelligence, but more showpersonship.

This show business aspect is nowhere more evident than in the current prevalence of digital assistants. On the face of it, Cortana appears a far cry from Microsoft's much-maligned animated paperclip of previous years and Amazon's Alexa appears to possess a wealth of knowledge and the ability to impart it in real time, creating the illusion of dialogue with a human. Siri, as the most popular voice assistant for mobile devices, adds a further dimension of immediacy, since interacting with an automated assistant via a mobile phone possesses some of the hallmarks of a phone call with another human. Such interactions, however, are short-lived and woefully limited to predictable enquiries and the reproduction of web-based information drawn from a variety of sources. This by no way belittles the technical achievements in terms of voice recognition and speech output, but there is a vast difference between the appearance of intelligence and the level of processing required to create a readily accessible digital assistant which would be of benefit to the independent language learner.

Nowadays, it is standard practice for educational institutions to promote independent study in the form of project work and online research. In many cases, this is achieved through the incorporation of a course management system (CMS) into the teaching program. At tertiary level, the most popular package of this type is currently Moodle, a learning platform or learning management system (LMS) designed to provide teachers and learners with a platform for creating personalised learning environments. Essentially, this is a content delivery system but can also be used to deliver language lessons through independently sourced interactive learning programs.

There is indeed a wide range of language learning software now available, just as there have long been numerous audio-based language courses incorporating the listen-and-repeat technique and, to a lesser extent, video-based language courses. The review below considers four of the most popular language learning programs at the time of writing and it is worth noting at the outset, that these computer-based language courses were not exclusively designed to teach English, but are each available for a number of target languages.

Rosetta Stone

Rosetta Stone is a well-established learning system which has successfully transitioned from its early CD-ROM format to online delivery. It features a fairly advanced speech recognition system and is based on the concept of immersive learning. The focus is on encouraging the learner to speak, but the absence of translanguaging features can present a considerable barrier to the autonomous learner.

Babbel

Babbel is somewhat more minimalistic in design but incorporates a module-based teaching method that goes beyond basic vocabulary training and provides courses tailored to the learner's individual language needs and drawing on the user's native language. Also featuring voice recognition, the system aims to guide the learner quickly towards clearly contextualised real-life conversations.

Duolingo

Duolingo is a relative newcomer in the field and is rapidly gaining in popularity. Unlike Rosetta Stone or Babbel, Duolingo draws heavily on gamification, aiming to provide learners with a fun experience that makes learning competitive and addictive. Competing to reach the top of the week's community leaderboard provides a new incentive to the goal of learning new items of vocabulary and improving grammar skills.

An uncomplicated lesson interface together with audio output and playful icons provide a pleasant experience, but the concept falls short of a fully developed language-learning package. The system provides an enjoyable way of learning basic vocabulary, but does not aim to promote conversational interchange and is severely limited by its lack of grammatical explanation or contextualisation.

Memrise

The distinguishing feature of Memrise is its extensive use of video sequences designed to demonstrate how native speakers use the target language in real-life situations.

A pronunciation trainer enables the learner to record and compare their vocal output with predefined audio examples, but any such system is only as good as the speech recognition tool it employs.

The content is firmly contextualised to make the learning experience feel more relevant and authentic, but in some ways, the system has many of the characteristics of an advanced flash card tool rather than an immersive language learning application.

In essence, all these language learning systems are advanced variations on the expert systems discussed in the main body of this study. The refinements are impressive and greatly enhance the learner experience, but the underlying approach is the same.

What has changed significantly is not the approach to developing learner-based systems, but the sheer volume of language input material available to the learner in a hyper-connected world. The ability to access a wealth of text, audio and video material online provides the autonomous learner with a powerful tool that by far surpasses the benefits of any particular automated learning system.

Indeed, it is this vast resource base that creates the impression of wisdom in digital assistants. Let us consider, for example, what Google Assistant actually does. In response to a spoken enquiry, it parses the query, identifies a key term and then googles it. The user can generally achieve exactly the same result by entering a text query and reading the result. The only real difference lies in the nature of the user interface. Modern software developers are, of course, aware that people habitually initiate spoken interaction in a more flexible manner then when creating a text query. Consequently, they are careful to avoid the traps that early programmers fell into and are in a position to define suitable responses to a range of humorous or awkward questions and user inputs. Ask a digital assistant to tell a joke and it will do so, pulling a random joke from a set of predefined options; ask for a fun fact and you will get one; ask about the meaning of life and you will get a witty answer. All this is possible because all of these things have been thought of before and can easily be parsed for. What is at work here is essentially the same approach as described in the main body of the present study. Deep down, nothing has changed. The mechanics of decision-trees and expert systems is still the same as it was at the time of the first edition of this book. Ironically, developments in voice recognition, text-to-speech (TTS) and other variations of speech output have heightened expectations

– and heightened expectations can lead to disappointment. And more complex decision trees create further hurdles for developers without necessarily improving outcomes.

The vast range of accent, intonation and speech patterns among native speakers present a particular problem here. Most users of speech recognition systems are familiar with the need for automated systems to be trained to accept the speech patterns of the individual user, but when applied to non-native speakers of English, the inherent problems are multiplied manyfold. Indeed, designing an input parsing system to understand non-native speech patterns can be counterproductive, since it may result in the system accepting as correct the very pronunciation features that may need correcting. Despite the vast number-crunching abilities of the fastest systems available, this remains a highly complex task, and when we factor in the myriad of variations among language learners from different backgrounds, it remains a potentially unsurmountable task.

Similar considerations apply to speech output. For example, if a text-to-speech system is being used to teach pronunciation, the question arises 'which pronunciation?', a topic which in itself is too vast to discuss here and to which there is no easy answer.

Having said that, both speech output and voice recognition are invaluable resources. Simply being able to ask a spoken question of a search engine app empowers the student to search through a wealth of resources with ease, but the results are the same as they would be with a text search.

There are so many reasons for optimism. As the high end of technologies enters the world of quantum computing and low-end systems offer access to virtual worlds, augmented reality and simulated real-time conversation, there are boundless opportunities for further development in the field of autonomous language learning, and consequently we might see ourselves as being on the verge of a major breakthrough.

As I now write in 2020, it would seem that this potential breakthrough is – more or less as it was over thirty years ago – just around the corner, but unfortunately, it never seems to arrive.

Appendix I

Telling the Time in German

As we enter the nineteen nineties, it is difficult to look back to a world without microcomputers, but as a reminder of the state of the art of the early nineteen eighties, here is a simple CALL routine written in the rather idiosyncratic ZX 80/TRS 1000 BASIC dialect. The initial question asking the time is in German since this is considered part of the task, but the feedback and control questions are given in English. For the sake of transparency, the text equivalents of the numerals are stored as individual variables. In a more advanced application, these would be stored as arrays or pushed onto a stack.

```
10 REM TELLING THE TIME IN GERMAN
20 REM MAURICE CLAYPOLE, MAY 1981
30 LET A$= "....."
40 LET H=RND(12)
45 LET M=RND(4)
50 LET C=O
55 LET D=O
60 CLS
70 IF NOT M=1 THEN PRINT H;":";M*15-15
80 IF M=1 THEN PRINT H;":";"00"
85 PRINT
90 PRINT "WIEVIEL UHR IST ES?"
100 PRINT
110 PRINT "ES IST ";A$;
120 IF M=1 THEN PRINT " UHR"
130 PRINT
140 PRINT
150 IF C>O THEN GO TO 300
160 INPUT A$
170 IF A$="S" THEN GO TO 900
180 LET C=C+1
190 CLS
200 GO TO 60
```

```
300 IF M=2 THEN LET M$="VIERTEL NACH "
310 IF M=3 THEN LET M$="HALB "
320 IF M=4 THEN LET M$="VIERTEL VOR "
330 IF M>2 THEN GO SUB 800
340 IF H=1 THEN LET H$="EIN"
350 IF H=2 THEN LET H$="ZWEI"
360 IF H=3 THEN LET H$="DREI"
370 IF H=4 THEN LET H$="VIER"
370 IF H=5 THEN LET H$="FUENF"
390 IF H=6 THEN LET H$="SECHS"
400 IF H=7 THEN LET H$="SIEBEN"
410 IF H=8 THEN LET H$="ACHT"
420 IF H=9 THEN LET H$="NEUN"
430 IF H=10 THEN LET H$="ZEHN"
440 IF H=11 THEN LET H$="ELF"
450 IF H=12 THEN LET H$="ZWOELF"
460 IF H=13 THEN LET H$="EINS"
470 IF H=1 AND M=2 THEN LET H$="EINS"
480 IF M=1 THEN GO TO 700
500 IF CODE(A$)=CODE(M$) THEN GO TO 530
510 PRINT "WRONG. TRY AGAIN."
520 GO TO 160
530 LET A$=TL$(A$)
540 LET M$=TL$(M$)
550 IF M$="" THEN GO TO 700
560 GO TO 500
570 PRINT "CORRECT. ANOTHER GO?"
580 PRINT "ENTER YES OR NO."
590 INPUT B$
600 IF CODE(B$)=62 THEN GO TO 10
610 STOP
700 IF A$=H$ THEN GO TO 570
710 GO TO 510
800 IF D=0 THEN LET H=H+1
810 LET D=D+1
820 RETURN
900 CLS
910 PRINT "DO YOU WANT TO START AGAIN?"
920 GO TO 580
```

From today's vantage point, it seems incredible that this was the full extent of CALL autonomy a mere ten years or so ago. As it stands, this routine just about fits into the ZX-80's 1K of memory, which is inadequate even to hold the data required for a 24-hour clock, let alone meaningful on-screen user instructions.

Furthermore, several programming language constraints had to be overcome. The maximum number of string variables in this dialect is 26, since each string may be designated only by a single letter plus the string sign. This is overcome by reassigning new values to M$ and H$ (minutes and hours). The screen blanks whenever the CPU is operating, making any animated display or time-lapse routine fundamentally impossible to design. The computer has no scroll facility, so it is necessary to distribute CLS instructions at appropriate points in any program to clear the screen and prevent an error function from occurring should the display exceed the maximum of 24 lines. On the ZX-80, user inputs cannot be made into a screen mask, but must be entered on an edit line below the output display. A user input can therefore only be combined with the computer output by subsequently refreshing the screen display.

Briefly, the program works by performing the following functions:

Line	Function
30-40	generate random values for hours (in the range 1 to 12) and minutes (1 to 4, representing the quarter hours).
50-60	set counters.
70-75	cause a random time to be displayed on screen in digital clock format (e.g. 2:45)
90-120	user prompt in the form of a question to student followed by a line to be completed, e.g.

2:45

WIEVIEL UHR IST ES?

ES IST .....

The student is now required to fill in the missing words (in this case, 'VIERTEL VOR DREI'). The user's input, whether correct or incorrect, will then be displayed.

120   Accounts for the linguistic anomaly by which the word 'Uhr' in German, like 'o'clock' in English, is used only with complete hours. The word 'Uhr' is therefore only added to the display if the time is on the hour, i.e. if M=I, e.g.:

2:00

WIEVIEL UHR IST ES?

ES IST ..... UHR

In this case, the student need only enter the correct number in German (e.g. 'ZWEI').

160   Using the same variable (A$) for the student's input as was used for the omission dots, enables the subsequent run to substitute the student's answer for the dots.

170, 900-920   Escape sequence.

200   Looping back refreshes display and substitutes student's answer for the omission dots.

300-490	Set string variables to solution
330, 800-820	In German, half past and quarter to are both expressed by reference to the following hour (half to and quarter to), therefore the value of H is incremented by 1 if the random time is half past or quarter to the hour.
460	Sets H$ to 'EINS' if the time displayed is 12:30 or 12:45 (i.e. 12 increased by subroutine 800 to 13).
470	Accounts for the illogicality by which one varyingly uses the neuter 's' on the word 'ein', e.g. 'ES IST EIN UHR' but 'ES IST VIERTEL NACH EINS'.
480	If the time is a full hour, then the correct student response consists of a single word and lines 500 to 610 may be bypassed.
500-600	Input parsing. If the time is other than a full hour, then the student's input should contain an expression corresponding to M$ immediately before the designated hour. The ensuing sequence overcomes the necessity for the student to make separate inputs for the minutes and the hour, which could be confusing and could distract from the learning process.
500	Checks the CODE (i.e. the Sinclair dialect numerical value assigned to the first

	symbol of a string expression) of A\$ to ascertain if it is equal to that of M\$. Subsequent lines use curtailing to check the remainder of the answer.
510,570	Inform student of success or failure and offer a further attempt or escape routine as appropriate.

Appendix II

Sample Run of King's Quest – Dialog Extract

After the initial title page, the user's character (Gwydion) appears in a hallway. After a period of inaction, a wizard appears in a cloud of smoke and then disappears again. The user has the options of moving his character about the environment, waiting for the computer to act first, or making a text input. The computer's vocabulary and linguistic ability are not known to the user. A heuristic approach is therefore required.

On this test run, the user waited for a considerable time, during which a wizard appeared twice in a cloud of smoke and then disappeared again. After moving his character about the hallway for a few minutes, the user attempted his first linguistic input. In the dialog extract below, non-text action (e.g. screen graphic response) is indicated in parentheses.

USER	MACHINE
look around	
	This is the main entry room of the wizard's house. The front door is to the south. Creaky stairs go upstairs and doorways lead north and east.
(moves about hallway)	
	"My office is dusty. clean it at once"
get duster	
	You don't need it.
clean the office	
	(wizard appears and disappears)
	How can you do that?
dust it	
	How can you do that?
go to the office	
	Just walk there.
(walks into office)	
	(display changes into interior of office)
look	
	Manannan is very private with his study and doesn't like you poking around. The huge oak desk is covered with his writing implements. An oak cabinet is in the corner. There is a chart on the rear wall. The bookshelves are filled with books on every subject. The wizard fancies himself to be quite a scholar.

(goes to the bookshelf)
look at book

> So many books line the bookshelf. You wonder when Manannan has time to read them all. Titles cover many subjects from ancient Arabic mythology and a study of the heavens to the philosophies of Socrates.

take book

> You glance at the titles of the books but do not see any that interest you. Wait, was that a glint of metal behind one large book?

move book

> You are not close enough.

look object

> It doesn't look interesting.

take object

> You don't need it.

read Socrates

> What's a Socrates?

read book

> How can you do that?

(goes to the desk)
sit down

> How can you do that?

look at the desk

The massive desk is made from oak. The wizard does all his reading writing and calculating here.

look at chair

The massive desk is made from oak. The wizard does all his reading writing and calculating here.

(magician appears)

"Gwydion, you were assigned a chore. You know what happens to lazy boys". Manannan shakes his head in disgust. "When will you learn to OBEY"? Up goes the dreaded finger. (screen character disappears in a cloud of smoke)

"Try hanging around in the kitchen a while, Gwydion", growls Manannan. (display changes to kitchen. Character is now hanging upside down above the fireplace).

You feel the blood rushing to your head as you realize that you are upside down. Straining to look up, you notice that your feet have been magically attached to a kitchen rafter. You struggle but can't release yourself. What a vexing situation!

jump down

You can't do that now. (written backwards)

(For a period of approximately five

minutes, all user inputs are ignored by the machine, which responds exclusively with this reversed message. Then, without warning, the user's character falls to the floor.)

You feel dizzy and nauseated at the sudden changes in body position. It is at least some consolation to find yourself on the floor again.

look

This is the kitchen of the wizard's house. Other than your own bedchamber this is the only place in the house that you feel you can call your own. The wizard rarely enters the kitchen. On cold days the fireplace is a cozy place to sit.

look at the shelf

The kitchen shelf holds many ingredients and kitchen implements for cooking. One useful item which catches your eye is the clay bowl you use for all of your mixing.

look at the bowl

It's just as it appears.

take bowl

You retrieve the clay bowl from the kitchen shelf and take it with you

take the bowl

You already have it.

take a Loeffel

> What's a Loeffel?
> (wizard appears)
> "Gwydion. I have decided to take a journey."
> (wizard disappears)

take a loeffel

> What's a loeffel?

its an instrument
for mixing

> What's a instrument?

a kind of tool

> What's a kind?

(takes the bowl

and goes to the table)

look at the table

> You use the heavy oak table when you prepare food for the wizard. Right now there is a loaf of bread, some fruit and a mutton chop on the table.

take fruit

> You take the fruit and carry it with you.

put the fruit in the bowl

> You don't need to put the fruit in the bowl.

eat the fruit

> Ok.

take the loaf of bread

> You take the loaf of bread and carry it with you.

cut the loaf in slices

> What's a slices?

cut the loaf

> How can you do that?

cut

> How can you do that?

take a knife

> You're too far away.

(moves to instrument rack near fireplace)
take knife

> You take the carving knife from the iron rack and take it with you.

cut bread

> You can eat the bread without slicing it.

(goes to the table)
cut meat

> How can you do that?

look

> This is the kitchen of the wizard's house. Other than your own bedchamber this is the only place in the house that you feel you can call your own. The wizard rarely

enters the kitchen. On cold days, the fireplace is a cozy place to sit.

look table

You use the heavy oak table when you prepare food for the wizard. Right now there is a mutton chop on the table.

cut chop

how can you do that

take chop

You take the mutton chop and carry it with you.

cut chop

You can eat the mutton without carving it.

look chop

This is a leftover mutton chop that the wizard hasn't finished. It still looks appetizing, though.

eat chop

Ok.

look knife

This knife is big enough and sharp enough to carve a large roast. (screen display blends in close up of knife.)

look fireplace

As it is now summer, the need to light a fire and cook hot food is diminished. The fireplace is, at the moment, not burning.

look rack

> There is an iron rack hanging on the wall by the fireplace. Your wooden serving spoon is hanging on the rack.

take spoon

> You take the wooden spoon from the rack and carry it with you.

look spoon

> This is a wooden kitchen spoon. (screen display blends in close up of spoon.)

(goes over to a collection of barrels.)
look

> This is the kitchen of the wizard's house ...

(breaks off game and saves same.)

Time elapsed approximately 30 minutes.

Appendix III

Abbreviations

AI	Artificial Intelligence
AL	Autonomous Learning
ALGOL	Algorithmic Language
BASIC	Beginner's All-Purpose Instruction Code
C	(a programming language)
CAD	Computer Assisted Design
CAEFL	Computer Assisted English as a Foreign Language
CAI	Computer Assisted Instruction
CALL	Computer Assisted Language Learning
CD-ROM	Compact Disc – Read Only Memory
CLOS	Common Lisp Object System
CMS	Course/Content Management System
COBOL	Common Business Oriented Language
COPSY	Contex Operator Syntax
CP/M	Control System for Microcomputers

CPU	Central Processing Unit
DOS	Disk Operating System
ED	Explanatory Database
EFL	English as a Foreign Language
ELT	English Language Teaching
ES	Expert System
FF	Fault Finder
Forth	(a programming language)
HC	Home Computer
HP	Hewlett Packard
HW	Hardware
IBM	International Business Machines
KB	Knowledge Base
KBS	Knowledge Base System
KE	Knowledge Engineer
L1	Human source language
L2	Human target language
Lisp	(a programming language)
LSB	Least Significant Bit
LMS	Learning Management System

MARS	Morphological Analysis for Retrieval Support
MCQ	Multiple Choice Quiz
METAL	(Siemens machine translation system)
ML	Machine Language
MS-DOS	Microsoft Disk Operating System
MSB	Most Significant Bit
MT	Machine Translation
NESC	Non-English Speaking Country
NL	Natural Language
OOSD	Object Oriented Software Design
Pascal	(a programming language)
PC	Personal Computer
PL	Programmed Learning
RAM	Random Access Memory
SW	Software
TINA	*Textinhaltanlyse* (text content analysis system)
TTS	Text To Speech
XPS	Expert System Shell

Appendix IV

References and Bibliography

Bartsch, R. & Vennemann, T., *Semantic structures*, Frankfurt: Athenäum, 1972.

Bernold, T. & Albers, G., ed., *Artificial Intelligence: Towards Practical Application*, Amsterdam: Elsevier Science Publishers, 1985.

Boden, M.A., *Artificial Intelligence and Natural Man*, Brighton: Harvester, 1977.

Boden, M.A., "Artificial Intelligence and Natural Man", in Bernold, T. and Albers, G., ed., *Artificial Intelligence: Towards Practical Application*, Amsterdam: Elsevier Science Publishers, 1985.

Chambers, A.B. & Nagel, D.C., "Pilots of the future: Human or computer?", in *Computer*, November, 1985, pp. 74-87.

Coburn, P. et al., *Practical Guide to Computers in Education*, Mass: Addison Wesley, 1982.

Cresswell, M. J., *Logics and languages,* London, Methuen and Co., 1973.

Curran., S. & Curnow, R., *Lernen mit dem Computer*, Niedernhausen: Falken Verlag, 1984.

Dakin, J., *The Language Laboratory and Language Learning*, London: Longman, 1973.

Eibl, G., "Current Work on Expert Systems and Natural Language Processing at Siemens", in Bernold, T. and Albers, G., ed., *Artificial Intelligence: Towards Practical Application*, Amsterdam: Elsevier Science Publishers, 1985.

Fischer, G., "Cognitive Science: Information Processing in Humans and Computers", in Winter, H., ed., *Artificial Intelligence and Man- Machine Systems*, Berlin: Springer Verlag, 1986.

Floegel, E., *Forth Handbuch*, Holzkirchen: Hofacker, 1982.

Higgins, J. & Johns, T., *Computers in Language Learning*, London: Collins, 1984.

Higgins, M., "Computer EFL Practice" in *Computers and ELT*, London: British Council Inputs, 1982.

Hoeppner, W., Morik, K., & Marburger, H., "Talking it Over: The Natural Dialog System HAM-ANS (No. ANS-26)", in *Research Unit for Information Science and Artificial Intelligence*, University of Hamburg, 1984.

Howatt, A.P.R., *Programmed Learning and the Language Teacher*, London: Longman, 1969.

Jensen, K. & Wirth, N., *Pascal User Manual and Report*, Berlin: Springer Verlag, 1976.

Kamp, H., "A Theory of Truth and Semantic Representation", in J. Groenendijk and others (eds.), *Formal Methods in the Study of Language*, Amsterdam, Mathematics Center, 1981.

Keenen, E., ed., *Formal Semantics of Natural Language*, Cambridge: CUP, 1975.

Kemmis, S. et al., "How do Students Learn?" in *UNCAL Evaluation Studies*, Norwich, 1977.

Krashen, S.D., *Principles and Practice in Second Language Acquisition*, Oxford: Pergamon Press, 1982.

Lehmann, E., "ISAR - ein experimentelles deutschsprachiges Faktenabfragesystem", in J. W. Schmidt (ed), *Sprachen für Datenbanken*, Informatik-Fachberichte 72, Springer, Berlin, 1983, pp. 11-25.

McCarthy, J., "Applications of circumscription to formalizing common sense knowledge", in *Artificial Intelligence*, 26/3, 1986, pp.89-116.

Newmark, P., *Approaches to Translation*, Oxford: Pergamon

Niedermair, G.T. et al., "MARS: A Retrieval Tool on the Basis of Morphological Analysis", in *Proceedings of the 3rd Joint BCS and ACM Symposium*, Springer, Berlin, 1984.

Noelke, U. & Savory, S. E., "Prolog-Systeme im Vergleich", in *Angewandte Informatik*, 1983.

Norman, D. A. & Draper, S. W., *User Centered System Design: New Perspectives on Human-computer Interaction*, CRC Press, 1986.

Papert, S., *Mindstorms*, Brighton: Harvester Press, 1980.

Partridge, D., *KI und das Software Engineering der Zukunft*, Hamburg: McGraw Hill, 1989.

Radig, B., "Design and Applications of Expert Systems", in Winter, H., ed., *Artificial Intelligence and Man-Machine Systems*, Berlin: Springer Verlag, 1986.

Raulefs, P., "Knowledge Processing Expert Systems", in Bernold, T. and Albers, G., ed., *Artificial Intelligence: Towards Practical Application*, Amsterdam: Elsevier Science Publishers, 1985.

RCA Corporation, *CMOS - A Programmed Text*, Somerville: RCA, 1984.

Rees, B., "Artificial Intelligence in a Large-Scale Enterprise", in Bernold, T. and Albers, G., ed., *Artificial Intelligence: Towards Practical Application*, Amsterdam: Elsevier Science Publishers, 1985.

Savory, S., "FF: A Nixdorf Expert System for Fault Finding and Repair Planning", in Bernold, T. and Albers, G, ed., *Artificial Intelligence: Towards Practical Application*, Amsterdam: Elsevier Science Publishers, 1985.

Schwarz, C., "Freitextrecherche - Grenzen und Möglichkeiten aus der Sicht der Informationslinguistik.", in *Nachrichten für Dokumentation*, 33/6, 1982, pp. 228-236.

Schwartz, D., "The Lisp Machine Architecture" in Bernold, T. and Albers, G., ed., *Artificial Intelligence: Towards Practical Application*, Amsterdam: Elsevier Science Publishers, 1985.

Simon, H. A., "Cognitive Science: The Newest Science of the Artificial" in *COGNITIVE SCIENCE* 4, 1980, pp. 33-46.

Tarski, A., "Der Wahrheitsbegriff in den formalisierten Sprachen" in *Studia Philosophica*, Vol. 1, 1935.

Tarski, A., "The concept of truth in formalized languages", in Woodger, J.H. (Trans.), *Logic, semantics, metamathematics* (2nd ed.), Oxford: Oxford University Press, 1956, pp. 152–178.

Turing, A.M. "Computing Machinery and Intelligence", in *Mind*, New Series, Vol. 59, No. 236, Oxford University Press on behalf of the Mind Association, 1950, pp. 433-460.

Wahlster, W. et al., "The Anatomy of the Natural Language Dialog System HAM RPM in *Natural Language Computer Systems*, Bolc. L., ed., Amsterdam, 1976.

Wahlster, W., "XTRA: Ein natürlichsprachliches Zugangssystem zu Expertensystemen" in: Deussen, P. (ed): *Sonderforschungs-bericht Künstliche Intelligenz*, Karlsruhe: Univ. Karlsruhe, 1984.

Wahlster, W., "Cooperative Access Systems", W. Wahlster in Bernold" T. and Albers, G., ed., *Artificial Intelligence: Towards Practical Application*, Amsterdam: Elsevier Science Publishers, 1985.

Wahlster, W., "The Role of Natural Language in Advanced Knowledge-Based Systems", in Winter, H., ed., *Artificial Intelligence and Man-Machine Systems*, Berlin: Springer Verlag, 1986.

Winograd, T., *Language as a Cognitive Process*, Mass: Addison Wesley, 1983.

Winograd, T., *Understanding Natural Language*, Edinburgh: The University Press, 1982.

Winston, P., *Artificial Intelligence*, Mass: Addison Wesley, 1981.

Winter, H., ed., *Artificial Intelligence and Man-Machine Systems*, Berlin: Springer Verlag, 1986.

Zadeh, L. A., "Test-Score Semantics for Natural Languages and Meaning Representation Via PRUF," in B. B. Rieger, ed., *Empirical*

Semantics, Vol. 1, Bochum, Germany: Brockmeyer, 1982, pp. 282-349.

Zadeh, L.A., "Outline of a Computational Approach to Meaning and Knowledge Representation Based on the Concept of a Generalized Assignment Statement" in *Proc. Of the Intern. Seminar on AI and Man-Machine Systems*, ed. Thoma, M. & Wyner, A., Springer, 1986, pp. 198-211.

www.ingramcontent.com/pod-product-compliance
Lightning Source LLC
Chambersburg PA
CBHW070441090426
42735CB00012B/2435